WELCOME

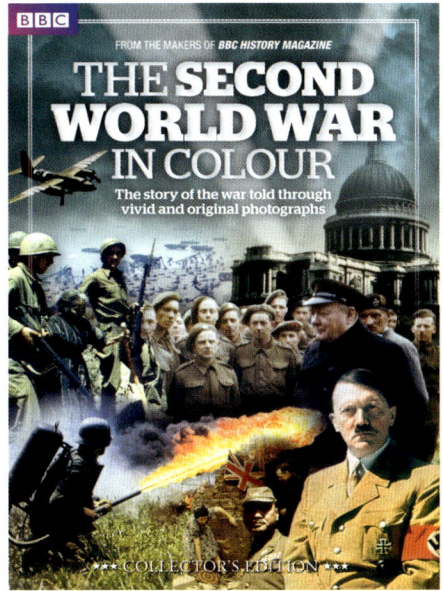

> The story of the Second World War has been told many times over – so often, in fact, that it can be difficult not to become immune to the realities of the conflict and how it affected ordinary men, women and children all around the world.

The original colour photographs that we've selected for this special edition of *BBC History Magazine* have a way of reopening our eyes to the brutalities of a war that took an estimated 66 million lives between 1939 and 1945. Somehow, the colour makes it feel much more modern, as if it could have happened yesterday.

Of course, the problem with attempting to tell the story of the war through colour photographs is that it is next to impossible to cover all the theatres and belligerents equally – there simply aren't any surviving colour photographs, to our knowledge, of events in Burma, for example. Similarly, there are far more surviving quality photographs of US troops in the Pacific than Japanese. However, as far as is possible, we have done our best to represent all areas of the war. Any aspects not represented here haven't been overlooked, there just weren't the necessary pictures to tell the story properly.

Don't forget that you can get more great history photography and writing every month in *BBC History Magazine*. Turn to page 112 for details of how to subscribe, or simply pick up a copy at your newsagent.

I hope you enjoy this special issue!

Rob Attar
Editor

CREDITS

EDITORIAL
Editor-in-Chief **Paul McGuinness**
Editor **Rob Attar**
Production Editor **Mel Woodward**
Subeditor **Rebecca Candler**
Editorial Assistant **Emma Jolliffe**
Editorial Consultant **Ashley Jackson**

ART & PICTURES
Art Editor **Sheu-Kuei Ho**
Designer **Lisa White**
Picture Editor **James Cutmore**
Picture Researcher
Rhiannon Furbear-Williams

PRESS AND PUBLIC RELATIONS
Press Officer **Carolyn Wray** 0117 314 8812
carolyn.wray@immediate.co.uk

CIRCULATION / ADVERTISING
Circulation Manager **Rob Brock**
Advertising Director **Caroline Herbert**

PRODUCTION
Production Director **Sarah Powell**
Production Co-ordinator **Emily Mounter**
Reprographics **Tony Hunt** and **Chris Sutch**

PUBLISHING
Publisher **David Musgrove**
Publishing Director **Andy Healy**
Managing Director **Andy Marshall**
Chairman **Stephen Alexander**
Deputy Chairman **Peter Phippen**
CEO **Tom Bureau**

Like what you've read?
Email us at bookazines@immediate.co.uk

© Immediate Media Company Bristol 2013. All rights reserved. No part of *The Second World War In Colour* may be reproduced in any form or by any means either wholly or in part, without prior written permission of the publisher. Not to be resold, lent, hired out or otherwise disposed of by way of trade at more than the recommended retail price or in mutilated condition. Printed in the UK by William Gibbons Ltd. The publisher, editor and authors accept no responsibility in respect of any products, goods or services which may be advertised or referred to in this issue or for any errors, omissions, misstatements or mistakes in any such advertisements or references.

PICTURES SUPPLIED BY GETTY, AKG, ALAMY, BRIDGEMAN, CORBIS, IMPERIAL WAR MUSEUM, MARY EVANS PICTURE LIBRARY, PRESS ASSOCIATION, REX FEATURES, SCIENCE & SOCIETY, TOPFOTO

BBC History Magazine 3

Anti-aircraft searchlights seek out enemy bombers in the night sky as the war is fought just on land and at sea, but in the air.

CONTENTS

6   **THE PATH TO WAR**
What were the complex and varied causes that brought the world to war?

10   **1939**
Hitler's territorial demands in Europe cause Britain an France to declare war, and the fighting begins.

18   **1940**
German forces sweep across mainland Europe, fighting hits the Mediterranean and Britain braces itself for the Blitz.

30   **1941**
The war goes global, as Hitler invades the Soviet Union, and Japan attacks both China and the USA.

46   **1942**
The United States has joined the conflict, the war in Africa begins to turn, and the horrors of the Holocaust step up.

62   **1943**
Trouble for the Axis, as they suffer major defeats in the USSR, the Atlantic, Africa, Italy and the Pacific.

78   **1944**
The invasion of Normandy on D-Day signals the beginning of the end of the war in Europe.

96   **1945**
The last months of the war see intense fighting in Europe and the dropping of atomic bombs on Japan.

114   **PARTING SHOT**
The war is over – but how will the world begin to pick up the pieces left by such a devastating conflict?

Nazi gathering

3rd October 1937
Bückeberg

Crowds estimated up to a million-strong gather at the annual Nazi Erntedankfest – or harvest festival – at Bückeberg, south of Hamelin. Such gatherings help Hitler build a mass support for Nazi causes.

THE PATH TO WAR

The period between the wars saw political differences, economic depression and anti-semitism create conflict in Europe

The path to war was a long and complex one, taking in a number of conflicts and political systems around the world.

It has been argued that the restrictions placed on Germany by the Treaty of Versailles, which signalled the end of the First World War, made the Second World War inevitable, but this would be over-simplistic.

During the 1920s, extremist politics rose in popularity, with Communism and Fascism both drawing strong support in mainland Europe. The power wielded by the new Soviet Union stoked fears among non-Communists that the Marxist-Leninist doctrine would spread, which only served to strengthen the hand of the Fascists opposed to Communism. Meanwhile, territorial disputes led to rising tensions. Tempers flared in Italy over ownership of its northeastern border areas, while Germany was keen to reunite the country with its people in areas such as the disputed Sudetenland, placed within Czechoslovakia by the 1919 Treaty of Saint-Germain. Civil war broke out in Spain in 1936, following an attempted coup by the fascist-leaning General Franco.

The unsteady global economy added to tension, too. The collapse of the US stock market in the late 1920s brought about a period of high unemployment and poverty. Hitler's Nazi Party rose to power in Germany in the first half of the 1930s thanks to support from Germany's right, who aimed to use the Nazis to eliminate Communism under the belief that they would be able to tame Hitler once they had helped him to power.

A global concern

In Asia, too, long-standing dissatisfactions led to confrontation. Japanese imperialism had long hoped to dominate China in order to fulfil its own ambitions and relieve the pressures of economic depression. The second Sino-Japanese War broke out in 1937. The 1941 Japanese bombing of Pearl Harbor would see this conflict become part of the world war at large.

Back in Europe, anti-semitism had been brewing for much of the 19th century, and it was this ideology that formed the basis of Nazism. In 1933, Jews were banned from holding various positions of office. Two years later, Jews were stripped of their rights. But the public outcry at the 1938 burning of synagogues and deportations of Jews to concentration camps convinced Hitler that the solution to the 'Jewish problem' must be dealt with outside of Germany itself.

By 1938, the Berlin-Rome Axis had seen a power-shift in Europe. Hitler annexed Austria and made claims on the Sudetenland. Keen to avoid another war, Britain and France accepted these actions, on the proviso that Hitler would make no more territorial demands. When, in March 1939, he invaded Czechoslovakia, Britain and France pledged that any such action against Poland would meet immediate military opposition. **H**

Nuremberg rally
◀ **10th September 1937,** *Nuremberg*
Hitler salutes the vast crowds at the 1937 Reich Party Conference. The Nuremberg rallies were a key date in the Nazis' calendar, offering perfect propaganda opportunities while cementing the most fervent support.

THE PATH TO WAR

Portrait of the Führer
▲ *The Berghof, Obersalzberg, Bavaria*
This photograph of Adolf Hitler was taken at his residence at the Berghof, near Berchtesgaden in the Bavarian Alps. During the 1930s, the Berghof became something of a notorious tourist hotspot, with Germans flocking in large numbers in the hope of catching a glimpse of the Führer.

Chamberlain arrives in Germany
▼ **28th September 1938,** *Munich*
British Prime Minister Neville Chamberlain is greeted by Nazi dignitaries on arrival in Munich. He is there to meet Hitler and discuss German threats to invade Czechoslovakia. On his return to England, he announces that he has secured "peace for our time." He believes the Munich Agreement would put an end to Hitler's plans for aggression, concluding: "Go home and get a nice quiet sleep."

Krystallnacht
◀ **9th November 1938,** *Bielefeld, Germany*
A synagogue in Bielefeld burns on Krystallnacht – the Night of Broken Glass. The pogrom, or series of attacks, was carried out against Jews in Germany and Austria. More than 1,000 synagogues were burned and thousands more Jewish businesses destroyed.

8 BBC History Magazine

THE PATH TO WAR

Homecoming parade
▲ **October 1938: *Sudetenland***
Ethnic Germans living in the disputed Sudetenland salute Nazi staff cars and fly Nazi banners as German troops occupy the former Czechoslovakian area.

Fighting talk
◀ **28th April 1939: *Berlin***
Hitler addresses the Reichstag in Berlin in response to a letter from US President Roosevelt in a speech lasting some two and a half hours.

BBC History Magazine 9

Call to arms

25 August, *Paris*
With the prospect of war becoming ever more likely, Britain and France begin mobilising troops in anticipation. This couple say goodbye, not knowing when, or even if, they would meet again.

1939

Following the invasion of Poland, Britain and her allies declared war on Germany, while the persecution of the Polish Jews began

At 11.15 on the morning of 3rd September, British Prime Minister Neville Chamberlain addressed the nation through BBC radio. "This morning the British Ambassador in Berlin handed the German Government a final note stating that, unless we heard from them by 11 o'clock that they were prepared at once to withdraw their troops from Poland, a state of war would exist between us. I have to tell you now that no such undertaking has been received, and that consequently this country is at war with Germany."

Air-raid sirens went up, and many feared that this new war would be fought by chemical and germ warfare, as well as fierce bombing raids. Yet it would be months before the Blitz would begin, or before any major military action was seen.

But while this 'phoney war' period may have been relatively uneventful in Britain, Nazi forces were causing devastation in eastern Europe.

The German-Soviet Treaty of Friendship partitioned Poland, and the German round-up of Polish Jews and activists began, which would lead to the ghettoes. By the end of the war, 6 million Poles would die – half of them Jews.

Lightning strike
◀ **September, Poland**
In the small hours of the morning of 1st September, 1.5 million German troops and 1,500 aircraft launched the first 'blitzkrieg' – or lightning war. The Polish army was soon overwhelmed by this new tactic of swift and devastating attack.

TIMELINE

15th January
Orders are given to the German army to prepare to occupy Czech lands.

30th January
Adolf Hitler tells the Reichstag that a second world war would lead to "the annihilation of the Jewish race in Europe".

15th March
Czech president Emil Hácha submits to threats and Germany is invited to occupy and protect Czechoslovakia.

17th March
In a speech in Birmingham, Prime Minister Neville Chamberlain asks of the occupation of Czechoslovakia: "Is this, in effect, a step in the direction of an attempt to dominate the world by force?" He confirms that Britain will resist any such move "to the utmost of its power".

1939

Shallow grave

September, *Gydnia, Poland*
Makeshift graves overlook the Polish port of Gydnia. Following occupation, the Nazis renamed the city Gotenhafen, and quickly rounded up any West Slavic ethnic Kashubians, executing around 12,000.

1939

Sign of the times
▲ *September, Poland*
The German sign reads 'Danger – do not proceed', as refugees clog the road during the German invasion.

The Porajmos
▶ *Vienna, Austria*
Romani families are registered ahead of deportation to Poland. Estimates as to how many Romanis were murdered by the Nazis in the Porajmos – the Romani Holocaust – range from 200,000 to 1.5 million.

TIMELINE

23rd August	25th August	1st September	3rd September	10th September
Germany and the Soviet Union sign a non-aggression pact. They also agree to a division of Poland.	Britain and Poland sign the Agreement of Mutual Assistance to help one another in the event of attack.	Germany invades Poland. Heavy attacks the length of the border lead to swift German military advances.	Britain and France declare war on Germany. The 'phoney war' begins.	Some 158,000 troops of the British Expeditionary Force leave for France.

A hero's welcome

▶ **November,** *Warsaw, Poland*
People gather at the foot of the monument to Polish hero Jan Kilinski in Warsaw's Krasinski Square. The monument is soon removed by the Nazis and hidden in the vaults of the National Museum. Within days, a message is daubed on the museum's walls: 'People of Warsaw, here I am! Jan Kilinski.' The statue would be returned to the square in 1945.

Better safe than sorry

Gas masks were distributed to all British citizens in 1939 and throughout the war, although the feared chemical attacks they were to defend against never came.

1939

Escape to the country
◀ *Instow, North Devon*
Throughout the war in Britain, children were evacuated from industrial cities to new homes with families in remote country areas.

Ready, coming or not
▼ *The south coast of England*
Britain went on immediate standby as soon as war was declared, yet it would be many months before German planes would cross the Channel.

TIMELINE

17th September
Soviet troops invade Poland from the east. Ten days later, Warsaw falls. By 6th October, Poland is defeated.

4th November
The Warsaw ghetto is established, with all the city's Jews being forced to live in one small part of the city.

30th November
The Soviet Union invades Finland, signalling the start of the Winter War between the two nations.

13th December
The battle of the River Plate. In one of the few actions of the so-called phoney war, British ships attack the German pocket battleship *Graf Spee*, which retreats to neutral Uruguay. Two days later and beyond repair, its commander scuttles the ship and takes his own life.

BBC History Magazine 17

German success

15 May, *Rotterdam, Netherlands*
Thirty thousand civilians are killed during the German bombardment of Rotterdam. The attack leaves 78,000 homeless. Paratroops swoop in to seize strategic locations and the Netherlands quickly falls.

1940

German forces invaded western Europe with relative ease and prepared for victory, but the British weren't about to give up

On 14th May 1940, Germany launched a heavy aerial attack on Rotterdam, before swiftly advancing on the ground. Similar attacks would continue across mainland Europe, with France falling by early summer.

In June, Italy declared war on Britain and France, transforming the war in the Mediterranean and north Africa. By July, British troops had evacuated from Dunkirk and Hitler was preparing his troops for a swift conclusion to the war. The key to this would be a negotiation with the British, who declined his offer of a surrender.

The German Navy was hesitant to do battle with the feared Royal Navy, and the Battle of Britain failed to destroy the RAF in the way that the Germans had hoped would clear the way to invade.

Hitler was forced to change his tactics and began a nine-month bombing campaign against several British cities. Designed to force the Allies into a peaceful solution, the brutal attacks spurred on the newly appointed, highly determined British prime minister, Winston Churchill.

By December, the US had pledged its support to the Allied forces – Germany was in for a very tough fight. **H**

German advance
◄ **May, Rotterdam**
German troops roll through the destruction during the brutal attack on Rotterdam. The key to the swiftness of the attacks is the use of radio equipment, which the Germans deploy to great success.

TIMELINE

8th January
Britain introduces rationing to conserve vital resources. Bacon, butter and sugar are the first items on the list.

9th April
The invasions of Denmark and Norway begin. The Germans target Norway to control its mineral resources, and use it as a springboard for further attacks. During the fighting, Germany and the British each lose approximately 3,700 men.

10th May
Germany's assault on the Netherlands, Belgium, France and Luxembourg begins.

10th May
Winston Churchill succeeds Neville Chamberlain as British Prime Minister.

BBC History Magazine 19

1940

Bomb site
▲ **May, Rotterdam**
Rotterdam lies in ruins after a huge onslaught of bombs. German troops move towards northern France and the Allies are unaware just how great a threat the enemy poses.

Norway invasion
▶ **April, Norway**
Germany makes an attack on Norway. The Germans see Scandinavia as a strategically vital, and the success of the campaign takes the Allies by surprise.

27th May–4th June

The British Expeditionary Force is evacuated from Dunkirk. Around 338,000 British, French and Belgium troops are rescued when Germany cuts off all land escape routes. An estimated 933 craft are hastily pulled into the mission, including motorboats and fishing boats.

28th May

After 18 days of fighting, Belgian troops are pushed back towards the sea, leading to Belgium's surrender.

10th June

Norway surrenders to German forces after two months of desperate resistance.

10th June

Italy declares war on Britain and France. Eleven days later, Italian troops move up to the French border.

New tactics

April, *Norway*
German paratroops descend against the icy backdrop of Norway. Airfields are secured and transport planes aid Germany in gaining quick control. The Germans would use this tactic again, a few weeks later in Belgium.

1940

Romani round-up
◀ **18th May,** *Germany*
On 27th April, Heinrich Himmler issues a decree demanding the rounding-up and deportation of all Romani families.

Unknown journey
▶ **May,** *Germany*
Families of Romani and Sinti descent are now seen as 'racially inferior' by the Nazi party. They are loaded onto trains for deportation, uncertain of their fate.

TIMELINE

14th June
German troops enter Paris. Thousands of Parisians have already fled by car, train or foot.

2nd July
Operation Sealion: German troops are ordered to begin planning for an invasion of Britain, starting at the south-eastern coast of England. This would be a last resort if a political solution couldn't be found.

10th July
The Battle of Britain: British and German fighter planes engage over the English Channel. Germany is much more confident in the air than against the Royal Navy and Hitler believes if he can destroy the RAF, an invasion of southern England is possible.

1940

Avenue of destruction
▲ **June, Dunkirk, France**

German forces press forward into France and the Allies are in trouble. Troops holding the British line of Arras are ordered to "fight to the last man and the last round".

Left behind
▶ **June, Dunkirk**

Although some 220,000 British and 120,000 French and Belgian troops were evacuated, some were less lucky, such as these prisoners captured by the Germans.

Hitler in Paris
▶ **23rd June, Paris**

Hitler takes a tour through Paris and drives down the Champs Élysée. During his only visit to the French capital, he is said to be pleased that Paris surrendered before any damage was done to the stunning architecture. Near the end of the war, he orders it to be burned to the ground.

19th July
Hitler assures Britain he has no desire to destroy its Empire, and offers a voluntary surrender. Britain swiftly declines.

3rd–6th August
Following rigged elections, Latvia, Lithuania and Estonia become Republics of the Soviet Union.

19th August
Italian troops enter British Somaliland. The Empire troops are evacuated to Aden.

23rd August
Hitler gives permission to bomb Central London. It is the first instance of bombing through the night.

25th August
British bombers retaliate by attacking Berlin. Though hard-pressed, Britain is never close to collapse.

1940

Propaganda specialists

25 July, *Dunkirk*
German troops are readily available to shoot material for propaganda films. The hasty evacuation from Dunkirk is seen by Minister of Propaganda, Joseph Goebbels, as the perfect opportunity to portray the Allies as weak and nearly beaten. He will continue to make films even when facing inevitable defeat.

1940

Airborne battle
▲ *South coast of England*
A German Messerschmidt chases a British Spitfire through the clouds above England. Over the next four months, Germany unsuccessfully attempts to destroy the RAF.

Icon of the skies
▲ Pilots discuss tactics while crewmen look over a Supermarine Spitfire. While the Hawker Hurricane took a great deal of the responsibility in the Battle of Britain, the Spitfire became the iconic fighter in the public's eyes.

The Blitz
▶ *September, London*
London is attacked for 57 days in a row and has 18,800 tons of bombs dropped on it. German leaders think this will force Britain to come to a negotiation.

TIMELINE

7th September

The Blitz begins in London. On the first day, 300 aircraft drop more than 300 tons of bombs on London's docks and the busy East End. By 5 October, there have been 18 major air assaults against the city, with many more to come.

27th September

Germany, Italy and Japan sign the Tripartite Pact – an agreement between the three nations to stand by one another during political, economic and military battles. Japan hopes this new alliance will intimidate the US and limit its involvement in Asian affairs.

28th October

Italy invades Greece and is now seen as having the largest and strongest navy in the Mediterranean.

Still standing

St Paul's Cathedral
While hundreds of buildings are destroyed around it, St Paul's Cathedral stays resilient against the German enemy. The survival of the iconic building becomes a symbol of hope and courage among the British.

Britain burning

Fire brigades work around the clock to tackle the 20,000 incendiary bombs dropped by the Germans. By the end of the Blitz, the bombing has killed around 40,000 people and destroyed one million houses.

1940

Fighting back
◀ **September,** *London*
Fireboats battle flames across the Thames. Mass destruction caused by the Blitz is designed to break British morale, but has the opposite effect.

The clean-up
▶ **September,** *London*
Neighbourhoods and communities are left in ruins. Around 2.5 million Anderson bomb shelters have been produced for householders, but there are still a great many civilian casualties nonetheless.

TIMELINE

14th November
A bombing raid on Coventry kills 554 people, provoking public outrage and leaving a lasting legacy.

9th December
The first major campaign in the Western Desert, Operation Compass, is launched by the Allied forces. The Italians are taken completely by surprise and after two days their Egyptian camps have been overrun. Troops are forced out and many surrender.

29th December
US President Roosevelt makes his "arsenal of democracy" speech, pledging to support the Allies by sending military supplies. It allows the US to provide military support and supplies while staying out of the fighting. Pearl Harbor was to be bombed a year later.

Trail blazers

Yugoslavia
German troops drive into a Yugoslav town, supported from above by the Luftwaffe. As with most of the country, the soldiers meet little resistance. Yugoslavia is a key stepping stone for the Nazis.

1941

As the year began, war raged in Europe and north Africa, but by the end of 1941, the conflict had spread around the world

Two years in, the war was primed to go global. The struggle of both Allied and Axis powers to secure resources for their war efforts ensured that the Balkans, Middle East and the USSR became targets of the conflict.

The Axis powers stormed ahead with their plans. Hitler prepared for his Soviet invasion and conquered Yugoslavia, Greece and Crete. Meanwhile, the Germans also assisted the Italians in Libya and Egypt. There, General Rommel's troops fought bitterly with the British, putting Allied control of the Suez Canal under threat.

In June, Hitler launched his invasion of the USSR: Operation Barbarossa. Millions of Axis troops were pumped into the country, making huge gains over the summer, and as winter arrived they neared the capital, Moscow.

With the Allies distracted by Germany's actions, Japan mobilised. In July, Japanese forces entered Indochina and not long after, the island nation launched its attack on Pearl Harbor. The US was left with little option but to declare war.

By December, the Axis's actions had delivered the Allies two formidable weapons: the US's military might and the USSR's seemingly infinite manpower. H

Out in the cold
◀ **March, Hungary**
Hungarian troops defend the Danube on a bitterly cold March day. After witnessing the destruction that the Nazis brought to Poland, Hungary submits to Hitler's rule at the end of 1940. Bulgaria follows suit in early 1941, and Germany gains all three countries without losing a single soldier.

TIMELINE

22 January
The Libyan port of Tobruk surrenders to the Allies, denying the Axis a crucial supply base in north Africa.

7th February
Despite greater forces, the Italians surrender Benghazi, Libya, to the British, and 20,000 prisoners are taken.

25th February
With his Indian division, Allied General Cunningham captures Mogadishu, capital of Italian Somaliland.

7th March
Allied air and ground forces arrive in Greece. Some have come from north Africa, where the line is weakened.

11th March
US President Franklin D Roosevelt signs the Lend-Lease Act, and the US begins to supply arms to the Allies.

BBC History Magazine 31

1941

The road to Athens
▲ **April, *Greece***
German troops march into Greece from the north. The Axis army efficiently forces the Allied line back taking Athens, in the south, by the end of the month.

Unforeseen consequences
▲ **April, *Greece***
Many of the vehicles used in Germany's Grecian attack rack up high mileages as they cross the country. When they are next used to invade the USSR, mass maintenance is a serious hindrance.

Going down with the ship
▼ **24th April, *Salamis harbour, Greece***
Many Grecian ports are targeted by the German Stuka dive bombers, including Salamis harbour, where the *Kilkis* battleship of the Royal Hellenic Navy is sunk.

TIMELINE

6th April	10th April	17th April	9th May	27th May
Yugoslavia and Greece are invaded by German, Italian and Bulgarian forces, capturing Athens on 27th April.	The siege of Tobruk begins: Allied troops remain trapped until 7th December.	After 11 days of fighting – including air raids that kill 17,000 civilians in Belgrade – Yugoslavia surrenders to the Axis.	Royal Navy captures *U-110* off Iceland. An Enigma machine is onboard – the find stays top secret for months.	The *Bismarck*, a battleship that has been targeting Britain's supply ships, is sunk by the Allies.

1941

Everyday sight
▲ **1st July, London**
As the Blitz continues, Britons get used to living in a warzone, and sights like this moored barrage balloon are commonplace. The balloons are tethered by metal cables, which hamper air raid efforts.

Attack from below
◀ Germany's U-boats are ruthlessly efficient tools of the war. The Nazis use teams of the submarines to target supply ships, in order to deprive Britain of crucial supplies. The boats remain submerged for days, waiting for the perfect moment to strike.

1941

On the warpath

June, *Soviet Union*
German infantrymen march into the USSR, as Hitler's Operation Barbarossa begins. The Nazi leader believes it will be a simple conquest, and initially the Germans make rapid and monumental advances, taking hundreds of thousands of Red Army troops as prisoners.

1941

Stoke the fire
▲ *Soviet Union*
On Soviet leader, Josef Stalin's command, the Red Army often sets fire to its own lands. Though extreme, the tactic restricts the Nazis' progress and even destroys an Axis command post.

Question time
◀ *June, Soviet Union*
Curfews, censorship and regular searches are commonplace under Nazi rule – with the threat of severe punishment, most individuals co-operate.

Hold the line
▶ *Soviet Union*
Armed with his hand grenade and gun, this Wehrmacht soldier guards a village in the perishing cold. He is one of around 4.5 million troops sent into the USSR by the Axis powers during Operation Barbarossa. The Soviets are aggressively resistant of Nazi occupation, so these guards are always on high alert.

TIMELINE

1st June
Britain helps install a pro-Allied government in Iraq. A week later, Allied troops enter Syria and Lebanon.

22 June
Operation Barbarossa begins as Germany invades the USSR. Italy and Romania also declare war on the USSR. Within the week, Finland and Hungary will declare war on the Soviets as well.

28th June
Germany captures 30,000 Red Army troops west of Minsk, before marching on to take the city.

3rd July
Soviet leader Josef Stalin issues a 'scorched earth policy' and fires are set to slow the German advance.

36 BBC History Magazine

Bleak midwinter

Soviet Union

When the coldest winter in 140 years hits Russia at the end of 1941, German troops are hopelessly unprepared for the hazards it brings. Many men develop frostbite, and their war machinery won't function in the icy conditions.
By 4th December, the temperature drops to an Arctic -35°C.

1941

Paying respects
▲ **July, China**
Chinese citizens look on as the bodies of those killed in an air raid attack by the Japanese are gathered in a makeshift morgue. Beginning in 1937, the Japanese carry out full-scale attacks on China. By the end of the war, the conflict kills around 10 million Chinese civilians.

All in one piece
▶ **July, Shanghai**
In the Yangtze river – not far from the US embassy – an American gunboat has survived a recent Japanese air raid on Shanghai. In December of the same year, Japanese forces occupy the city, forcing the closure of the consulate.

TIMELINE

3rd September
The gas chambers at the Auschwitz-Birkenau extermination camp are used for the first time.

8th September
The siege of Leningrad begins. It will last for 900 days. Estimates for the number of civilians who will die during the siege range from 640,000–800,000.

29th September
The massacre at Babi Yar. Thousands of Jews are rounded up and murdered by Nazi SS troops outside Kiev.

18th October
Japanese war minister Hideki Tōjō succeeds Prince Konoe to become the country's prime minister.

A leader divided

September
For Hitler, autumn brings tactical turmoil. His priority is the invasion of the Soviet Union, but his attentions are divided between two cities: the home of communism, Leningrad, and the capital, Moscow. He decides to besiege Leningrad, using as few troops as possible, reserving much of his military force for the battle over Moscow.

1941

Safety in numbers
▲ **North Africa**
German vehicles kick up dust as they travel in a mass convoy. This region sees an almost-constant turnover of victories and defeats, with the same morsels of land passing between Allied and Axis control many times over.

Desert life
▶ **September: north Africa**
German soldiers set up shelter in the hot, arid landscape of north Africa. This hostile environment becomes the backdrop for many bloody and fiercely fought battles.

1941

Roll call
▲ **February: Tripoli**
Hitler sends troops to Africa to assist his Italian ally, Mussolini. As the German Afrika Korps reports for duty, Generals Rommel (German) and Gariboldi (Italian) inspect the troops.

Smart solutions
▲ **North Africa**
Soldiers across north Africa have to make do with short supplies. This Afrika Korps serviceman, for instance, uses a magnifier to light his cigarette.

Back and forth
▶ **Near Sollum, Egypt**
This British base is a toughly fought-over piece of terrain. Occupation of the land swings between the belligerents over and over again – on one occasion, it stays in Allied control for just a single day.

BBC History Magazine 41

Surprise attack

7th December,
Pearl Harbor, Hawaii
While appearing to negotiate peace, Japan is in fact planning to attack. In November – while in peace talks with the US – Japan's six aircraft carriers set sail for Oahu, ready to unleash their torpedo bombers on the naval base's infrastructure, ships and planes.

1941

Island inferno
◄ **7th December, Pearl Harbor**
Over 360 Japanese bombers and fighters strike the base, destroying three US warships and 188 aircraft beyond repair. In the attack, around 2,300 Americans lose their lives, while only 55 Japanese die.

Up in smoke
▶ **7th December, Pearl Harbor**
After bomb and torpedo attack, black smoke pours out of the USS *California*. The *Oklahoma* is also capsized, and the *Arizona* is blown up.

TIMELINE

18th November
Operation Crusader is launched – after three weeks, British troops are freed from the siege of Tobruk.

26th November
Japanese ships head to Hawaii in secret. The US demands that Japan withdraw from the Axis.

7th December
Without declaring war, Japan bombs US naval base Pearl Harbor, as well as the Oahu airfields, Hawaii. While the fleet is crippled, the crucial aircraft carriers are undamaged. The next day, America and Britain declare war on Japan.

11th December
Though not obliged to, Germany and Italy declare war on the US, creating a genuinely global conflict.

BBC History Magazine 43

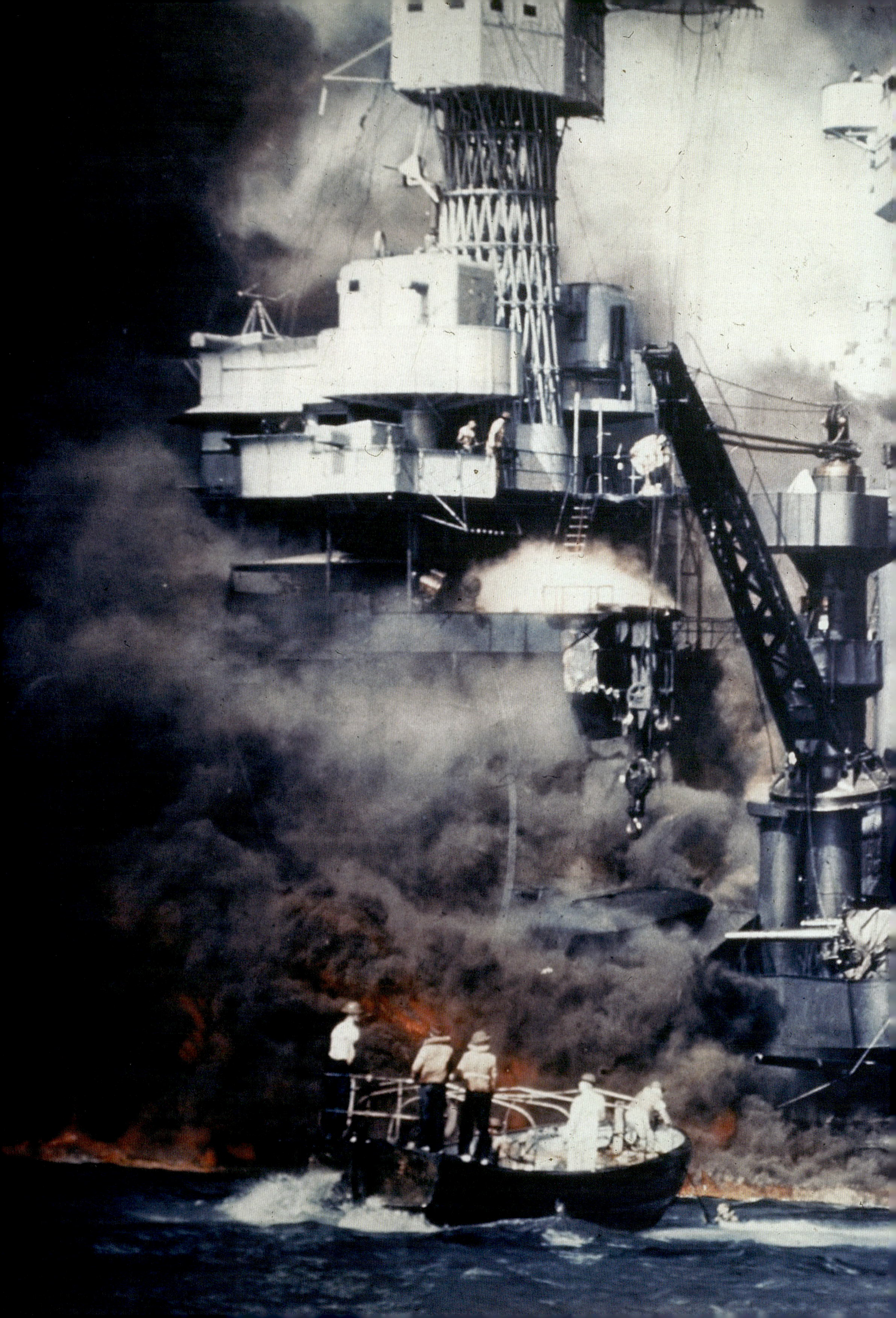

1941

Enter the US

7th December, *Pearl Harbor*

This destructive attack propels America and all of its industrial and economic reserves into the war. The day after the US fleet is crippled, the US Congress votes to enter a state of war against Japan, and Britain follows its Atlantic cousin soon after.

No mercy

March, *Lübeck, Germany*

A 600-year-old church lies in ruins after an air raid on the important German port, Lübeck. Strategic bombing is a key part of the Allies campaign – ports and industrial cities are significant targets.

1942

As the balance began to change, the Axis powers saw defeats in the Pacific and Africa. But not before victories of their own

With America now among the Allied ranks, the world was very much at war at the start of 1942. The first few months saw key Axis advances, but as the Allied forces developed their combined strategies, the balance would soon shift.

Against British, Dutch and US forces, the Japanese conquered many islands in the Pacific and huge areas of mainland Asia, including the conquests of Burma, Malaya and Singapore. But in late spring, Japan became increasingly overpowered by America's naval might. The battles of Coral Sea and Midway were decisive, though costly victories for the US. Thereafter, the US began to take back the Pacific islands, starting with Guadalcanal.

At Stalingrad, Operation Barbarossa reached a stalemate, as thousands of men fought bitterly over the ruined city. Meanwhile in north Africa, Axis and Allied forces battled for key locations. By the end of the year, Rommel had fled Egypt to Tunisia.

Despite suffering military setbacks, the Nazis pressed on with their anti-Semitic regime, with the completion of Auschwitz-Berkenau furtherer refining the process of the massacre of Jews and others seen as enemies of Nazism. H

British humiliation
◀ January
Burma
A convoy of trucks, transporting the Royal Engineers to Imphal, India, waits for the all clear at traffic gates. Outmatched by Japanese forces, in March, the British troops will abandon the capital, Rangoon, and retreat to India.

TIMELINE

2nd January
The Philippines capital, Manila, falls to Japan. The US and Philippine troops withdraw to the Bataan Peninsula.

11th January
Operation Drumbeat: Germany begins its attempts to destroy shipping across the east coast of America.

20th January
Reinhard Heydrich chairs a secret conference in Wannsee, Germany, to discuss the 'Final Solution to the Jewish problem'. After this, Heydrich industrialises the process, establishing efficient methods for massacre.

26th January
'Over paid, over sexed and over here': the first American troops arrive in Britain.

1942

Naval might

June, *Midway, Pacific ocean*
A US navy aircraft carrier is loaded with planes ready to battle a Japanese fleet. Led by Admiral Nimitz, the US emerges as the clear victor in the battle of Midway – 300 sailors and airmen from America's ranks are lost, as opposed to 3,500 from Japan's.

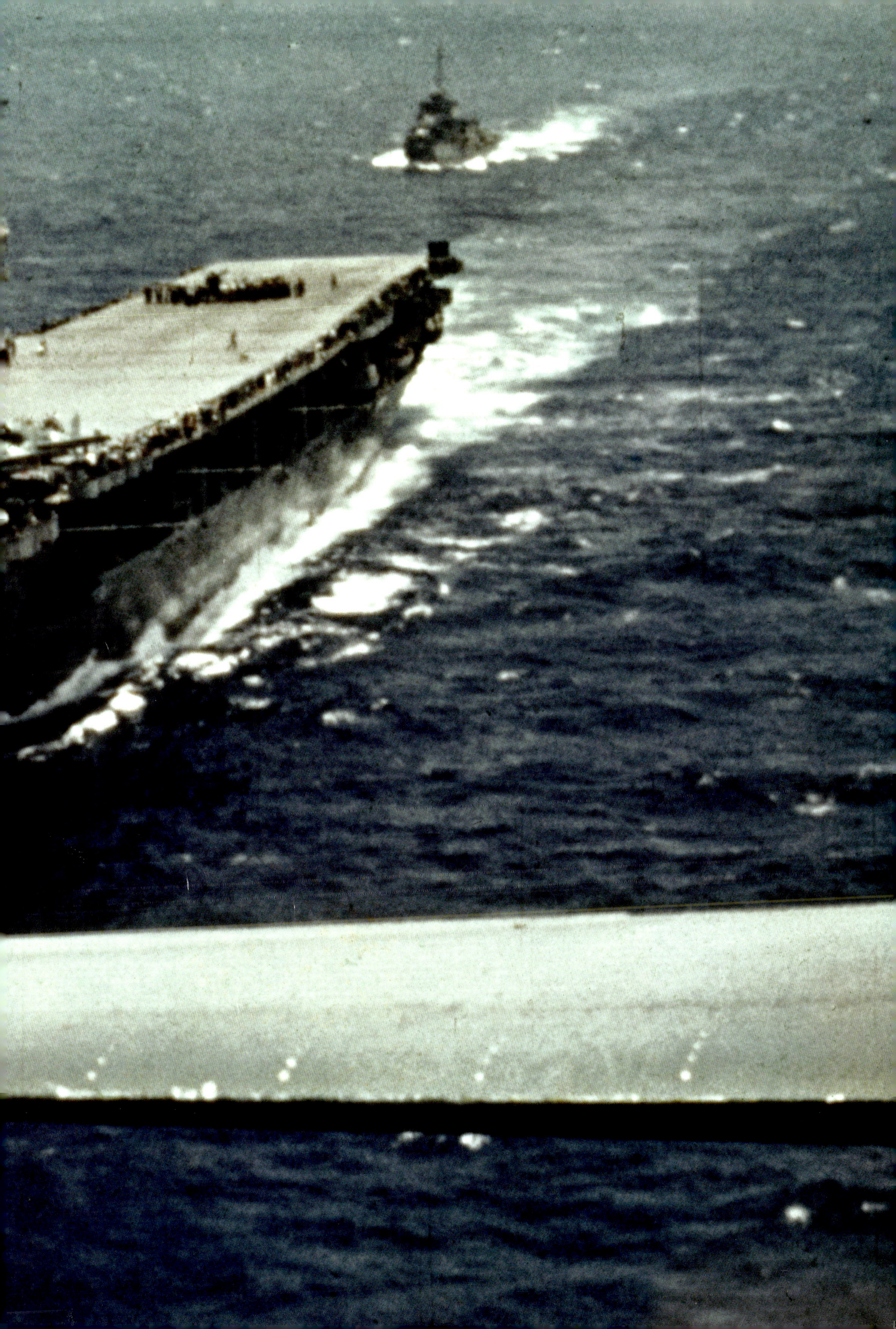

1942

Key victory
▲ *6th August, Guadalcanal*
On the eve of the Guadalcanal invasion, US warships gather in the Pacific. The next day, marines storm the island, and swiftly capture a Japanese airfield in mid-construction. On 20th August, the US will receive the first aircraft delivery.

Friendly fire
▲ *Soviet Union*
Two Wehrmacht soldiers lay down a Swastika flag, signalling their location to the German bombers – a basic tactic to minimise friendly fire.

Flames of destruction
▶ *Soviet Union*
A German soldier burns the Soviet landscape using a backpack flamethrower. These weapons are highly effective against tanks at close range.

TIMELINE

15th February
Around 70,000 Allied troops are captured by the Japanese as Singapore falls.

8th March
Japan takes the Burmese capital, Rangoon, after almost two months of fighting. The British forces withdraw to India.

20–23rd March
A British convoy suffers heavy losses after an attack from the Italians, as it nears its destination of Malta.

15th April
The islanders of Malta are awarded the George Cross by King George VI – Britain's highest decoration for civilian bravery. During March and April, Axis forces pound the island with twice the bomb tonnage that London endures through the Blitz.

50 BBC History Magazine

Barbed operation

Soviet Union

A German soldier cuts through barbed wire defences installed by the Soviets. The Germans are unable to emerge victorious against the USSR – despite their 4.5 million troops, they are still outnumbered.

1942

Ghetto children
Lodz, Poland
Jewish children line up for lunch in the ghetto, to collect a portion of their meagre starvation-level rations. As the Nazis develop their Holocaust strategies, deportation of Jews – including children – from the ghettos to extermination camps becomes increasingly frequent. By the end of the war, some three million Polish Jews will be exterminated.

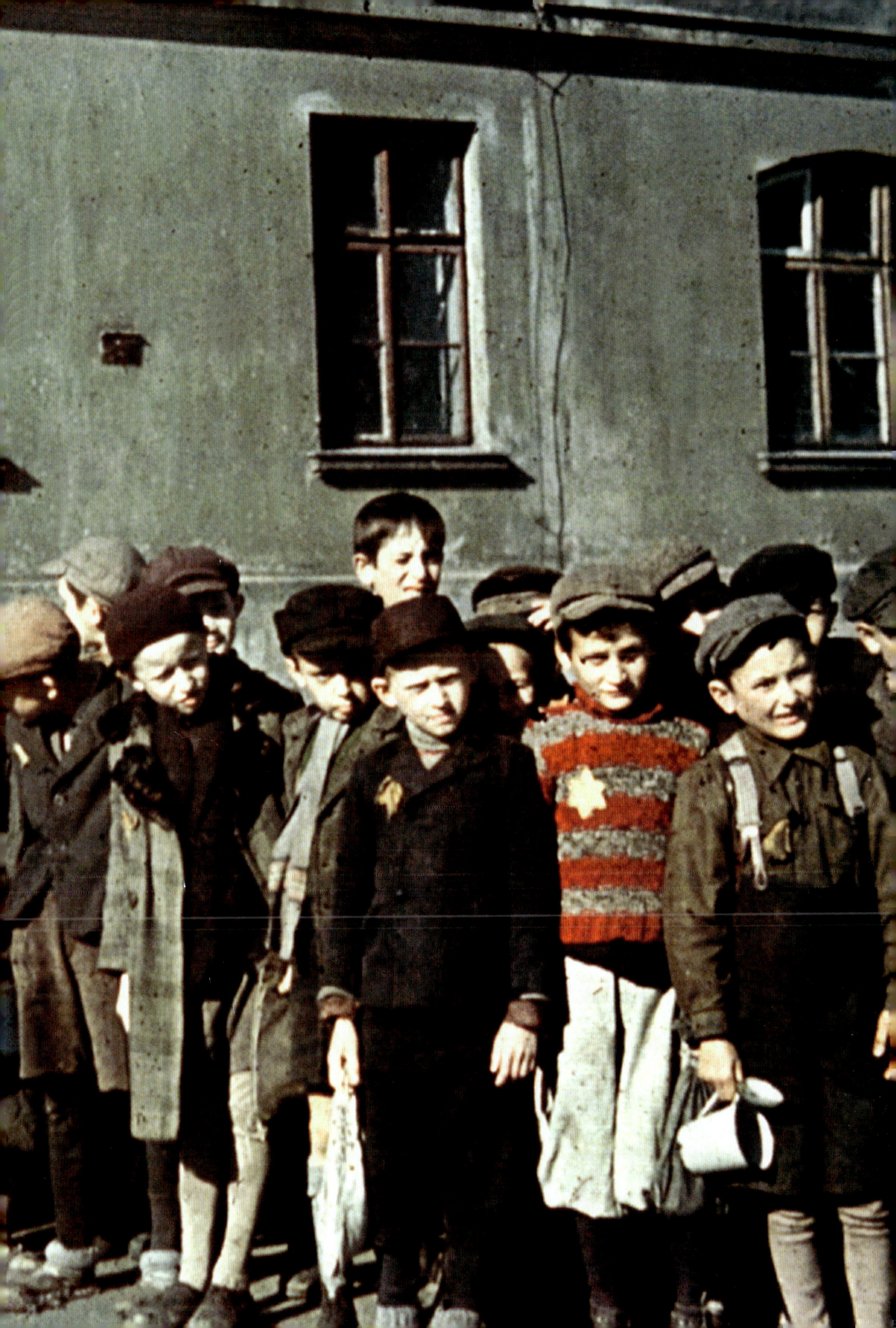

1942

Orderly living
▲ *Lodz, Poland*
Nazi ghettos are well organised – some inhabitants have jobs, such as delivering post, to keep them busy and controlled.

Two leaders
▶ *Lodz, Poland*
Heinrich Himmler – the man behind the 'Final Solution' – sits in his car at the Lodz ghetto. The white-haired man, Mordechai Chaim Rumkowski, is head of the Council of Elders at Lodz. He helps make it a centre of industry.

TIMELINE

30th May
Cologne, east Germany, suffers devastating damage from the RAF's first 1,000-bomber raid.

4-7th June
Enormous Japanese forces are outmanoeuvred in the battle of Midway, in the Pacific. The US fleet takes Japan's navy by surprise, destroying its aircraft carriers and forcing a withdrawal.

13th August
The Manhattan Project – the US development of atomic weapons – is given the green light by President Roosevelt.

23th August
German troops begin to enter Stalingrad, which has been devastated by intense bombing.

Behind the walls

Lodz, Poland
Ghetto inmates are forced to work in factories and workshops, to manufacture goods for Germany – especially for the SS. Because of this productivity, some men and women of Lodz survive long after the Jews of other Polish ghettos are massacred.

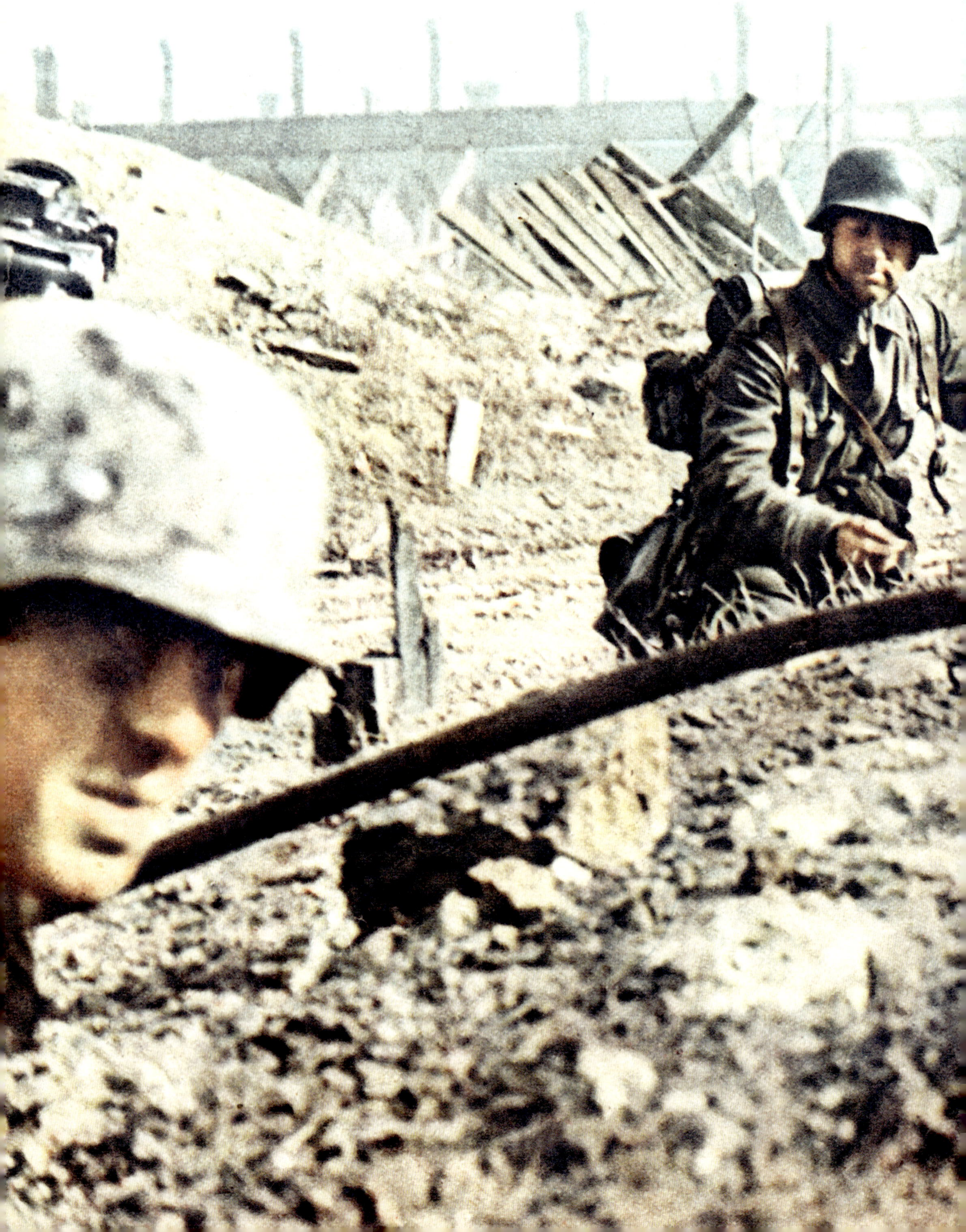

1942

A bitter battle

Stalingrad, Soviet Union
One of the most savage battles in the war, the conflict over Stalingrad sees hundreds of thousands of men sent to their deaths. After many months of fighting, the German 6th Army surrenders to the Soviets.

1942

Rough terrain
▼ *North Africa*
German Afrika Korps patrol the desert in a BMW R75 motorcyle, armed with a light machine gun. Between the two battles of El Alamein, Rommel's troops are restricted to a narrow 65km strip along the north coast of Egypt.

On the lookout
▲ *August, El Alamein, Egypt*
Wehrmacht soldiers patrol the desert. At the first battle of El Alamein in July, the British hold off a German advance.

Second bite
▶ *October, El Alamein, Egypt*
On 23rd October, Britain's 8th Army launches the second battle of El Alamein. Within a week, the Afrika Korps is reduced to 35 tanks from 520.

TIMELINE

30th August
Outside El Alamein, Rommel attacks the British 8th Army, but is forced to withdraw within two days.

12th September
At Guadalcanal, Japan's 17th Army is repelled by US marines at the battle of Bloody Ridge.

18th October
German soldiers now occupy most of Stalingrad, but the Soviets scrambles more troops.

23rd October
The Allies begin the second battle of El Alamein. Their victory is seen by many as a major boost for the Allies.

30th October
German code books are taken from the sinking U-559.

Observation station

North Africa
An Afrika Korps soldier searches for potential Allied movement – especially tanks – as he looks through rangefinding binoculars. Tank warfare is the most suitable form of battle on this open, often featureless desert landscape.

Flying the flag

August, *London*

After an air raid, a woman salvages board games from amid the wreckage. The Blitz may cause suffering and material damage, but it does not destroy morale, as Hitler had hoped. Instead, the British become more resilient and determined to strike back.

1942

Land girls
◀ *July, Suffolk, Britain*
Over 80,000 women join the Land Army during the war. As well as farming much of Britain's food, they also work on timber, manufacturing important supplies such as pit props for coal mines.

Sheltered life
▼ *August, Britain*
Sturdy Anderson shelters can be found in many British gardens. The hideaways offer reliable defence from German air raids, which continue over Britain until 1944.

Quick chop
▶ October, *Essex, Britain*
In between sweeps, an RAF pilot gets a haircut. Many fighters stay close to their aircraft while on duty, so they can take off as quickly as possible when a call comes in.

TIMELINE

8th November
Operation Torch: the Allies launch their invasion of north Africa, landing in Morocco and Algeria.

19th November
Operation Uranus: a one-million-strong Soviet force begins to surround the German 6th Army, led by General Paulus, at Stalingrad. By the end of January 1943, the Nazi troops surrender.

12th December
Operation Winter Storm: Germany attempts to relieve the surrounded 6th Army at Stalingrad.

21st December
Despite the failure of Operation Winter Storm, Hitler refuses to allow General Paulus to attempt a retreat.

Freshly picked

March, *St Mary's, Isles of Scilly*

Over 1,000 soldiers are stationed on St Mary's – it serves as a staging post for the battle of the Atlantic. Island activities, such as picking daffodils, make a nice change from training for the war-ready troops.

1943

The Allies began to turn the tide – as US and British forces took the initiative, they forced the Axis powers onto the defensive

It might have seemed that the Nazis started the year well, however, it soon became clear that his high point was passing: Germany would be defeated. The first sign was the surrender of Axis troops at Stalingrad, in February. Hitler faced further defeat in tank battle for the Soviet city of Kursk. And by the end of the year, the Axis had been forced out of Africa.

In the spring, the American and British troops forced the U-boats out of the Atlantic. With the route between Britain and the US clear, plans for D-Day could become a reality.

Over the summer, the Allied operation to invade Italy began as British, American and Canadian troops entered Sicily. Come September, they struck the mainland. But in the autumn, the Nazi forces struck back, maintaining a strong defensive line that effectively drew a line through the middle of the country.

The US continued to battle Japan, taking island after island in the Pacific.

Meanwhile in central Europe, the Holocaust continued apace, while German cities suffered heavy air raids. Hamburg, the Ruhr dams, Munich and even Berlin were all targets for Bomber Command.

Forging ahead
◀ **January, Casablanca**
Winston Churchill and other senior British figures gather in Morocco to meet with America's service leaders. Together, they plot the way forward. It is decided that the next target will be Sicily. With this island in Allied hands, the whole of the Mediterranean and a route into Italy would be open. The mission is code-named Operation Husky.

TIMELINE

27th January
The first US air raids on Germany take place – the cities of Emden and Wihelmshaven are bombed in the day.

31st January
Against Hitler's order, Field Marshal Paulus surrenders the 6th Army at Stalingrad.

2nd–4th March
Battle of Bismarck Sea: American B-25 bombers sink eight Japanese transport ships and four destroyers.

26–27th March
British General Montgomery attacks the Axis' Mareth Line in south Tunisia, forcing a retreat.

18th April
Admiral Yamamoto, the man who plotted the Pearl Harbor attack, is shot down by American fighters.

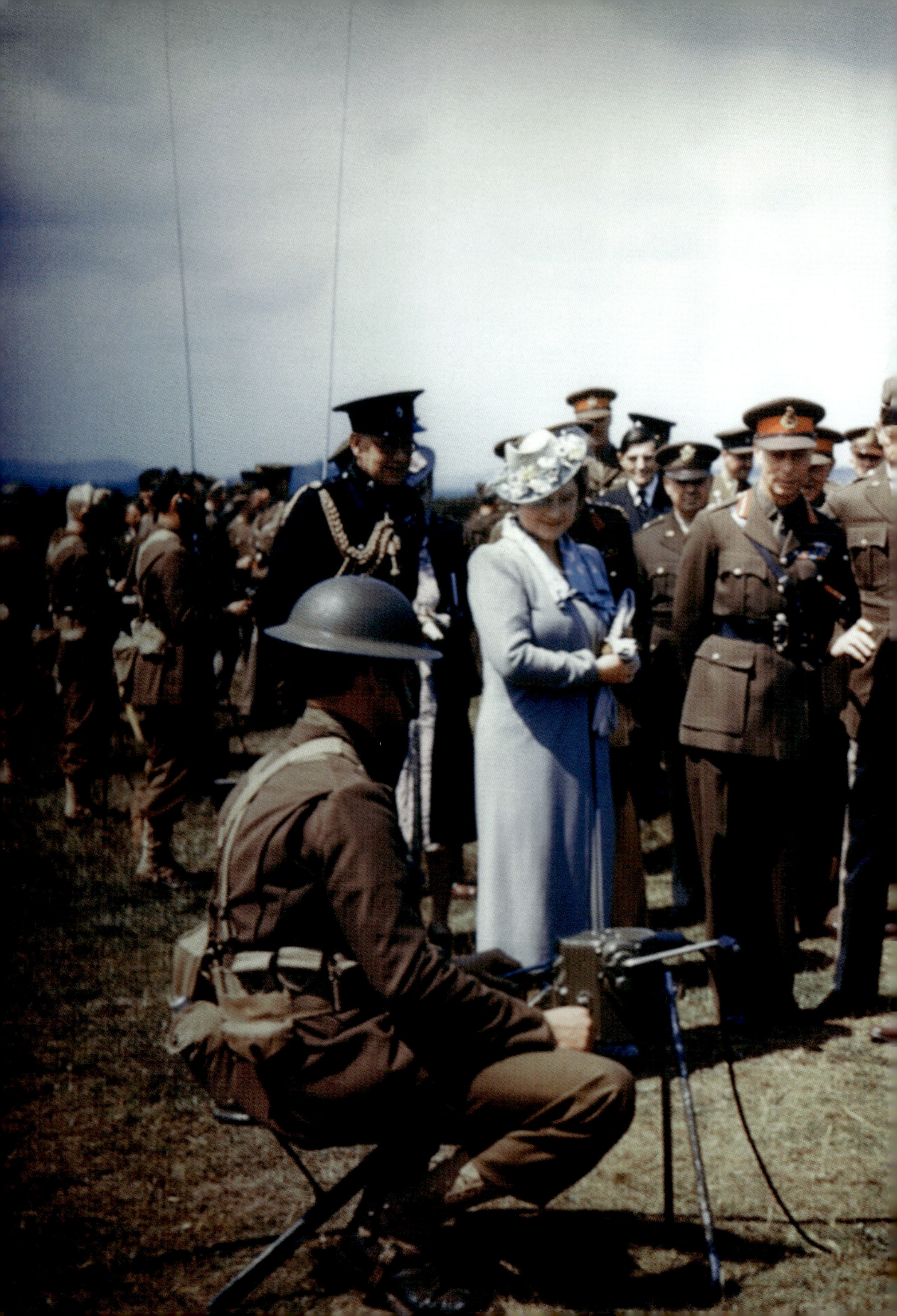

1943

A royal occasion

England
King George VI and his wife Elizabeth visit Allied troops. The British monarch often visited servicemen and women – later in the year, the king travels to north Africa, to meet soldiers at El Alamein. The couple's high profile earns them great popularity, and also makes them symbols of British resilience.

1943

Prison life
▲ **May,** *Tunisia*
Captured Axis soldiers wait in a temporary holding camp after the last Italian and German forces in Tunisia are defeated. Hitler anticipates the defeat, but is unable to pull sufficient reinforcements together in time.

Waiting games
▶ *Tunisia*
Axis POWs play cards in a military camp. The captured troops comprise eight different divisions. Without these men at his disposal, Hitler has no immediate way to defend Italy from an Allied attack.

TIMELINE

13th May
Allies take around 240,000 Axis prisoners of war as the Italian First Army surrenders in Tunisia.

16th May
The Dambusters Raid: two of Germany's Ruhr dams are breached by a new British creation, the 'bouncing bomb'.

24th May
After record losses, Karl Dönitz, commander-in-chief of the Nazi navy, pulls all U-boats out of the North Atlantic.

30th June
Operation Cartwheel: Rendova Island is the first to be captured in the US offensive to take the Solomon Islands.

13th July
Operation Citadel: After a nine-day battle over the Soviet city of Kursk the Germans are forced to retreat.

1943

City streets
◀ *Munich*

As the Allied offensive gains momentum, few German cities are spared from air attacks. In October, Munich is bombed twice in 48 hours, with both daylight and night-time raids devastating the Bavarian capital.

After the fire
▼ *July, Hamburg*

In four formidable raids code-named Operation Gomorrah, Bomber Command blasts Hamburg. Germany's most important port is all but obliterated, with some 40,000 civilian fatalities. Despite the destruction, the city begins to function again relatively quickly.

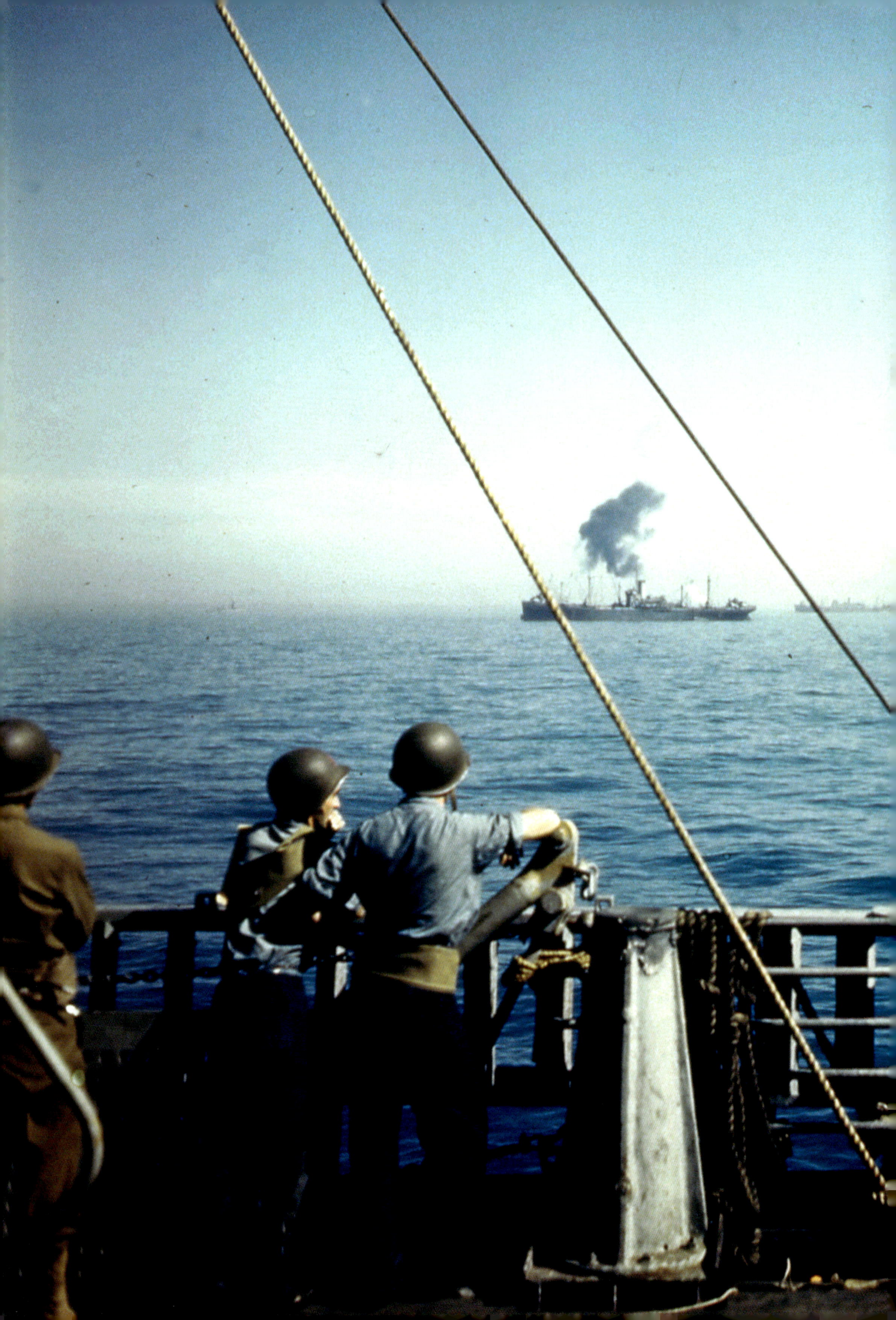

1943

Heading for shore

July, *Mediterranean sea, near Sicily*
Troops look on as Operation Husky – the Allied invasion of Sicily – gets underway. The operation is vast, requiring both amphibious and airborne assault. Here, other ships generate smoke screens, hiding the troops that are being ferried to the shore from potential aerial attack.

1943

Defensive attack
▼ **July, Gela, Sicily**

Clouds of thick black smoke pour out of an Allied ship, struck by Axis bombs during the invasion of Sicily. In total, Operation Husky costs the Allies nearly 25,000 casualties. Despite the losses, the island is captured in five weeks.

Steady progress
▶ **July, Gela, Sicily**

Allied forces make their way to the port city of Gela. On arrival, many US soldiers are welcomed by locals as if they are liberators, as the Italians have grown contemptuous of Mussolini's regime. On 24th July, the dictator is deposed and replaced with the pro-Allied marshal, Pietro Badoglio.

TIMELINE

10th July
Allied troops land in Sicily. The ambitious amphibious assault uses over 2,500 ships.

24th July
The start of a series of bombing raids on Hamburg. By 3rd August, over 8,000 tons of bombs are dropped.

17th August
During a bombing raid on a Messerschmitt plant in Bavaria, the US loses 60 bombers. Further losses during a similar raid in October cause the Allies to restrict bombing targets to those within the range of their escort fighters.

17th August
When Allied forces enter Messina, Sicily, they find the Axis troops have fled Sicily for the Italian mainland.

1943

Training mission
▲ **August,** *Britain*
Members of the Home Guard run through an exercise, practicing the art of camouflage warfare. Though the risk of a British invasion has diminished by this point, these passionate volunteers don't let their defences down.

Fire stoppers
◀ *London*
Women take emergency calls at a fire station in the capital. By the end of the war, over 43 per cent of the labour force is female, with as many as 6.5 million women taking jobs.

1943

Public notice
◀ **September, *Eastern front***
Wehrmacht soldiers study propaganda posters. Propaganda is a powerful tool used by every nation involved in the war. It can manipulate public opinion – the anti-Semitic flyer on the right links Stalin with Judaism.

Benito escapes
▶ **12th September**
Abruzzo, Italy
After he loses power in July, Mussolini is arrested and detained in the Appenine mountains. On 12th September, a German commando of gliders rescues the Italian ex-leader, delivering him to Axis territory in northern Italy.

TIMELINE

9th September
Allied forces push further into mainland Italy, landing at Salerno, where they come under heavy fire.

11th September
Germany takes control of crucial cities in northern Italy, among them Rome, Milan, Bologna and Verona.

12th September
Mussolini is rescued by German paratroops. On 18th September, he declares a new Italian Social Republic.

1st October
American forces enter and capture the city of Naples, Italy.

13th October
Under the leadership of Marshal Badoglio, Italy (south) joins the Allied forces and declares war on Germany.

Ghost town

September, *southern Italy*
A US Sherman tank rolls through a town that has seen heavy fire from Allied artillery. The Italian campaign slows to an excruciating pace after August, as rough terrain, poor weather and fierce German defence each take their toll on the mission.

1943

Sight seeing

November, *Naples, Italy*

After entering mainland Italy on 3rd September, slowly but surely, the Allies push the Axis forces further and further north, finally capturing Naples on 1st October. Here, US military trucks are parked next to Naples' Santa Lucia fountain (also known as the Fountain of the Giant), with Mount Vesuvius in the background.

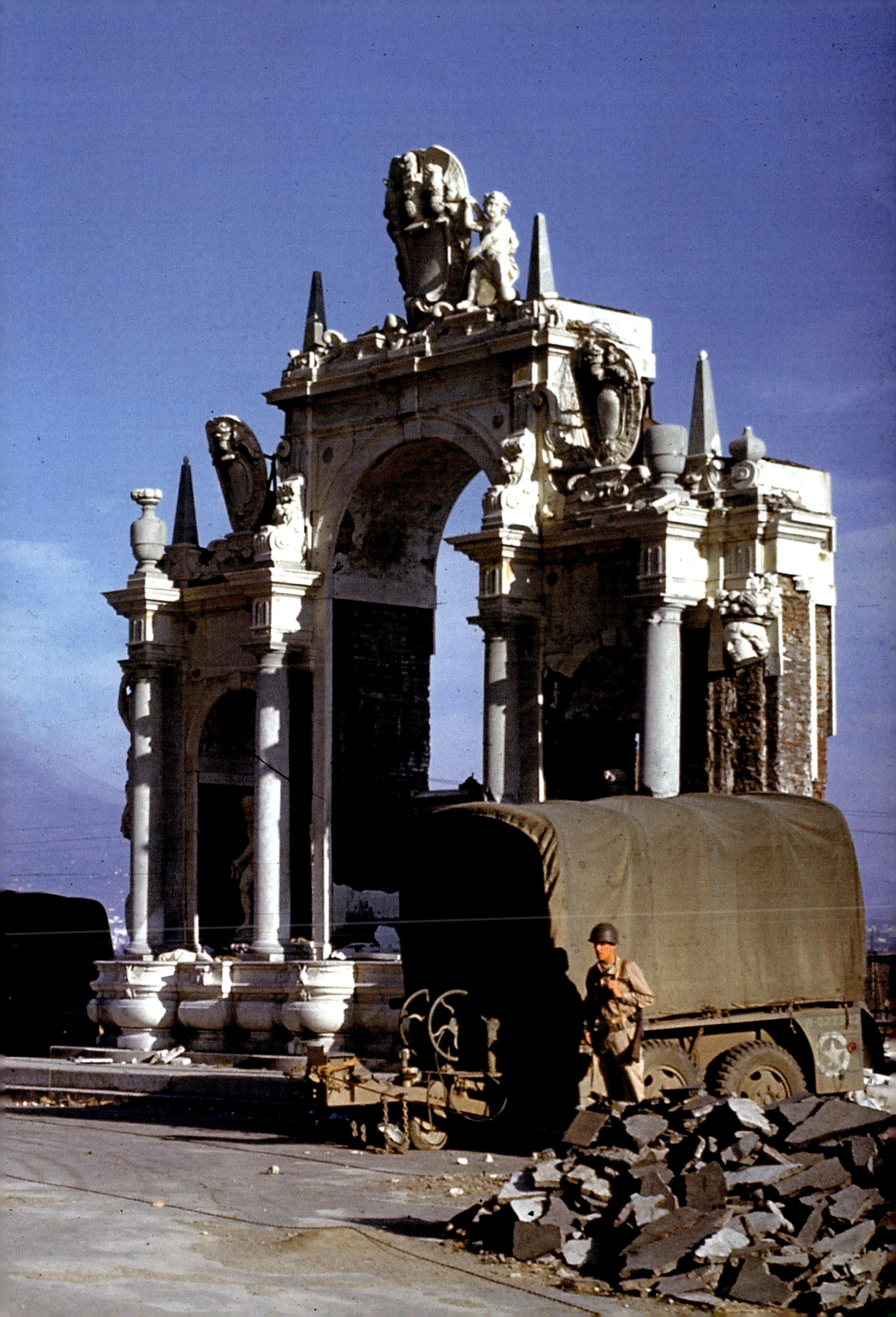

1943

Local knowledge
▶ **November, *Naples***

The Neapolitans are only too happy to welcome Allied troops. Before the Allies arrive, the citizens revolt against the Germans, and force them to withdraw from the city.

Bombing raids
▼ Crewmembers enjoy a laugh while checking their B-17 bomber in England. Over 120 US bombers were lost in two missions on munitions plants at Schweinfurt, Bavaria, in August and October.

Safety first
◀ US troops take care with bomb storage at a dump in England.

TIMELINE

4th November

Germany establishes the Gustav Line – a strong fortification spanning the width of Italy south of Rome. The Allies become embroiled in a costly struggle over the position, with no clear strategy for success.

6th November

Kiev is liberated by Soviet forces.

18th November

A campaign of intense bombing of Berlin begins. Over the winter, the raid kills or injures 14,000 civilians.

20th November

Operation Galvanic: US troops land on two of the Gilbert Islands, as the South Pacific offensive begins.

1943

Costly victory
▲ **November, Tarawa**
Despite heavy bombardments to diminish Japan's fortifications on the atoll, the US marines come under heavy fire as they land, suffering 3,300 casualties.

Bloody Tarawa
◄ **23rd November, Tarawa, Gilbert Islands**
US forces continue to advance across the Pacific. The hard-won victory at Tarawa leaves only 17 Japanese survivors out of 3,000 troops and 1,000 construction workers.

Battleships

Victory markings are applied to a destroyer in the Pacific. The crews of ships and planes took pride in their successes and triumphantly scored them for all to see.

1944

The Allies continued to dominate, with successes at the D-Day landings, eastern front, Philippines and Burmese campaigns

As 1944 began, the Allies were beginning to see a victorious end to the war in their sights. A successful push north through Italy saw the Germans pushed back to the Gustav Line. In Britain, generals were finalising plans for the invasion of Normandy that would come in June. On the eastern front, the Soviets cleared the enemy from the USSR before entering Poland.

In the Pacific theatre, General MacArthur's Allied forces from the US, Australia, New Zealand, the Netherlands and various Pacific Islands were making strategic advances and continued to make ground in the New Guinea campaign and Operation Cartwheel, with the aims of neutralising Japanese forces and establishing bases within range of Japan itself. The Japanese offensives in Burma were repelled, although the US was forced to withdraw bombers from China.

The invasion of five beaches in Normandy was key, and saw the Allied forces advance through northern France to the German border. However, the Germans had one last effort, launching a major offensive in the Ardennes. The battle of the Bulge proved costly to the Allies, but was no more than a delay on the road to Berlin.

Men of action
◀ **14th February**
D-Day commanders meet to discuss plans for the June invasion, including General Eisenhower, Supreme Commander of the Allied Forces in Europe (centre), and General Montgomery, who led the ground forces at Operation Overlord (on Eisenhower's left).

TIMELINE

22nd January
Allied troops land behind the Gustav Line at Anzio. However, fierce German defence traps them until summer.

12th February
The green light is given to Allied plans for the invasion of Normandy – Operation Overlord.

17th February
In a raid at Truk, in the Caroline Islands, US bombers destroy some 200,000 tons of Japanese shipping.

4th March
In Burma, the Japanese launch U-GO, a major offensive with a clear road to India as its goal.

15th March
The Allies pound the key Italian stronghold of Monte Cassino from the air and ground.

Flight deck

April, *New Guinea*
US planes prepare for take-off on the flight deck of the USS *Lexington*, en route to New Guinea. General MacArthur's New Guinea campaign from 1942–45 was one of the most decisive military campaigns of the war.

1944

Bridge over troubled waters
▲ **February, *Abruzzo, Italy***
US jeeps cross a trestle bridge in the Abruzzo region of central Italy. German defences on the Gustav Line prove difficult for the Allies to break down.

Ready for action
▶ **April, *Monte Cassino, Italy***
British soldiers man an anti-aircraft gun below Monte Cassino, the scene of a number of costly assaults between January and May, which leave up to 55,000 Allies and 20,000 Germans dead.

TIMELINE

18th April
A Japanese offensive into China forces the US to abandon a number of its air bases.

28th April
D-Day rehearsals turn tragic as German torpedoes attack US landing craft at Slapton Sands in south Devon.

15th May
The deportation of Hungarian Jews to Auschwitz begins.

23rd May
The break-out from Anzio begins, with the Germans retreating to positions south of Rome.

18th May
Following intense fighting, Polish troops hoist their flag on top of the monastery at Monte Cassino.

1944

Monastic ruins

Monte Cassino, Italy
Despite massive bombing, which destroyed the hilltop monastery, the Allies failed to dislodge the incumbent German troops. It wasn't until the fourth attempt that the Allies finally secured the strategic position overlooking the entrance to the Liri and Rapido valleys, part of the Gustav Line of German defence.

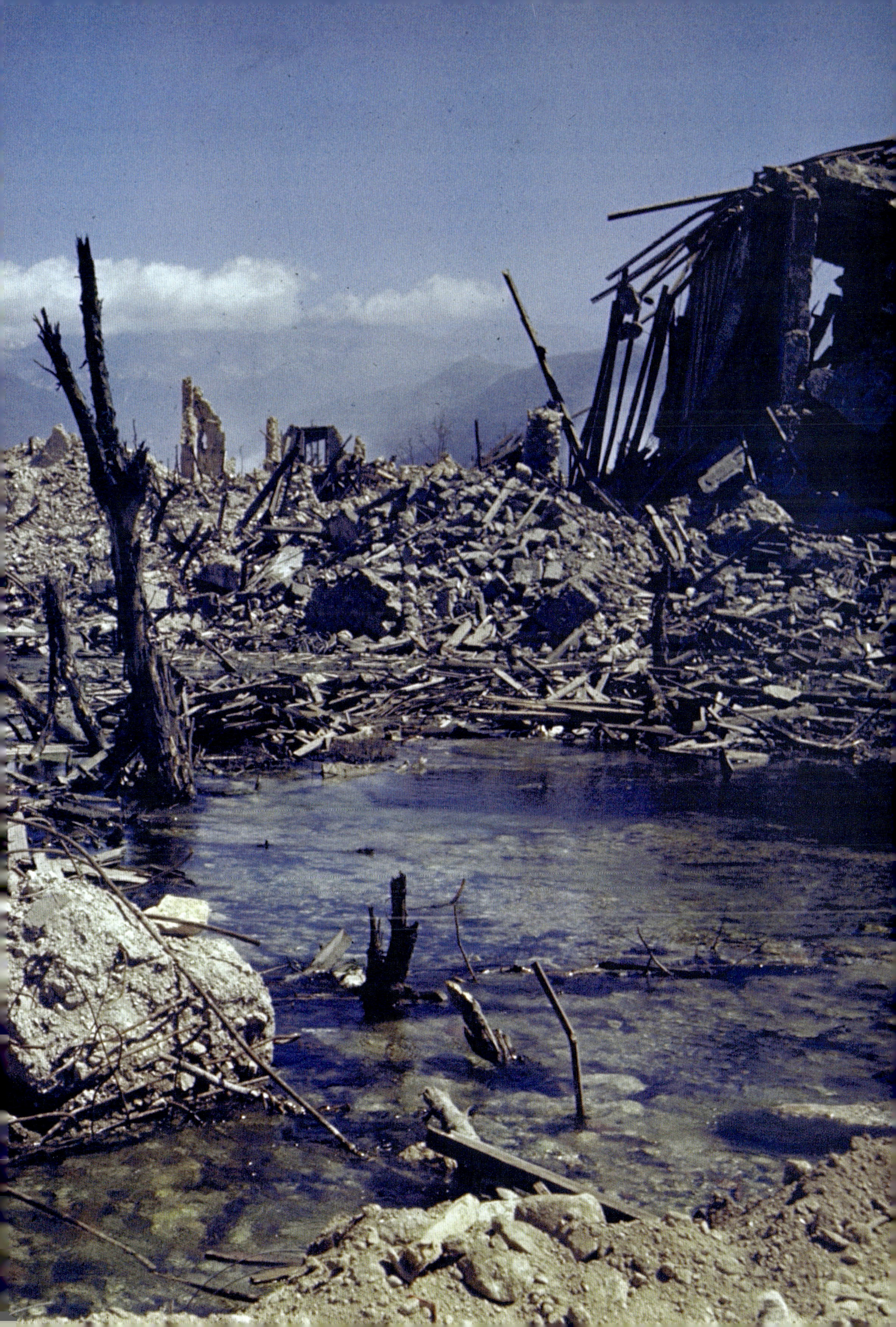

The fall of Rome

5th June, *Rome*

The day before D-Day, Allied soldiers gather in front of the Altare della Patria in Rome, which had been taken the day before. The monument holds the Tomb of the Unknown Soldier, built after the First World War.

1944

Ghetto clearance
▲ **July, Lodz, Poland**
The deportation of Jews from the Lodz ghetto to concentration camps gathers pace as the Nazis decide to liquidate the ghetto.

Gunning for victory
▶ **June, Saipan, Mariana Islands**
Cannon are brought into position during the battle of Saipan, which the US won in July. A defining moment in the war in the Pacific, the victory here means that US aircraft are now within striking distance of Japan.

TIMELINE

4th June
German troops are pushed back to north of Rome. The next day, Allied troops enter the city in triumph..

6th June
D-Day. After years of planning, Operation Overlord – the Allied invasion of France – takes place. Following paratroop drops behind enemy lines, British, American and Canadian forces land at five beaches, which are reasonably quickly secured to allow for heavy reinforcement. Over the coming weeks and months, Allied troops slowly advance inland, linking up to create a new front pushing towards Germany.

13th June
The first V-1 weapon is launched against Britain. Around 16,000 of these flying rocket bombs will be fired.

BBC History Magazine

1944

Off to war
◀ **5th June, Weymouth, England**
American GIs make their way towards their transport on the eve of the Normandy invasion – D-Day.

Wagons roll
▲ Amphibious trucks are loaded onto an American LST (Landing Ship, Tank) ready for use on the Normandy beaches.

A waiting game
◀ **June, Weymouth, England**
Troops load their trucks onto the transports ready for the D-Day landings. The organisation involved in coordinating the attack has taken months to put together. Now, the combined forces simply wait for the right weather forecast.

1944

Return flight
▲ **6th June, Normandy**
The battle of Normandy rages below as bombers and their escorts return home after their missions.

On the beach
▶ **6th June, Normandy**
Troops arrive to reinforce the initial wave that landed at the five Normandy beaches on the morning of D-Day.

TIMELINE

18-20th July
Operation Goodwood: British and Canadian troops launch an attack to the east of the strategic city of Caen.

20th July
Operation Valkyrie: a German Army attempt to assassinate Hitler and effect a coup is foiled. A bomb planted in the conference room at Hitler's Wolf's Lair headquarters fails to kill the Führer, and the conspirators are swiftly caught and executed.

25th July
Operation Cobra: American forces launch an offensive to break-out from the Normandy town of St Lô. The coming weeks will see fierce fighting from town to town as the Allies seek to secure northern France, and push eastwards to the German border.

1944

Turning point

6th June, *Normandy*
The invasion of Normandy on D-Day was a huge step on the road to victory in Europe within the next 12 months.

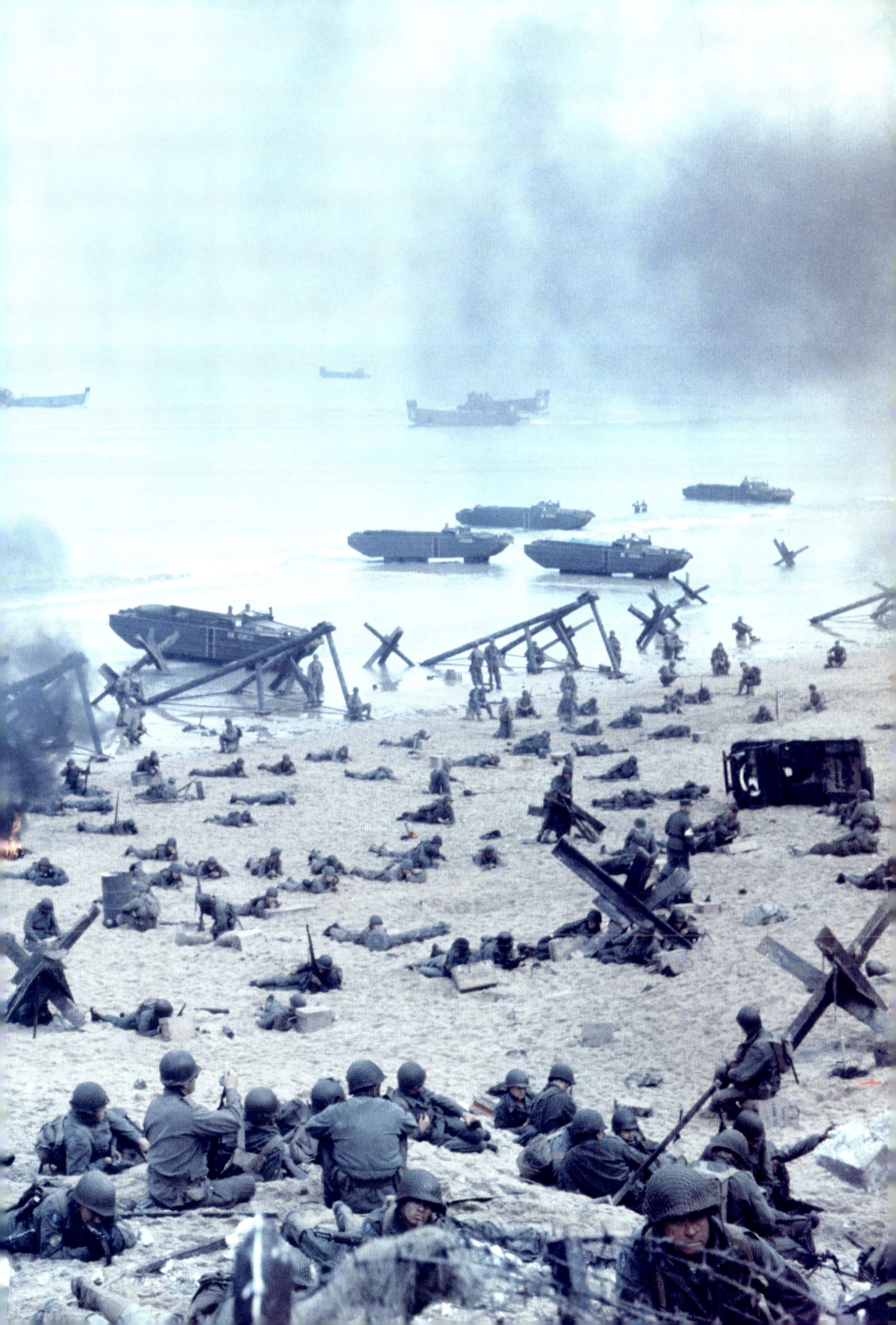

Capital of the Ruins

August, *St Lô, France*

The Normandy town of St Lô was virtually destroyed by Allied bombers during Operation Overlord. Many thought the destruction so great that the town, nicknamed the 'Capital of the Ruins', should never be reconstructed, but left as a permanent monument. One US soldier is reported to have commented ironically: "We sure liberated the hell out of this place."

1944

Wave of joy
▶ **August, *Normandy***
French civilians wave greetings as their liberators push across northern France.

Churchill's visit
◀ **22nd July, *Caen, France***
Field Marshall Montgomery peers over Winston Churchill's shoulder as the Prime Minister speaks to men of the 50th Division, who took part in the assault on D-Day.

TIMELINE

1st August
With the Red Army less than 20km away, Polish resistance fighters rise up against their German occupiers, and soon have control of much of the city. However, while Stalin isn't yet ready to liberate Warsaw, he also prevents other Allies supporting the Poles. The SS soon quash the rebellion, ruthlessly executing anyone suspected of involvement. Some 15,000 resistance fighters and 225,000 civilians are killed.

25th August
The liberation of Paris. Against Hitler's orders, German troops withdraw, leaving the city relatively intact.

20th August
The Soviets attack Romania, which is joined over the next month by Bulgaria, Finland and Estonia in surrender.

1944

'Vive de Gaulle'
▶ **26th August,** *Paris*

Crowds line the Champs Élysée to rejoice at the liberation. Even now, German snipers are still active and a number of people are shot dead amid celebrations at the Place de la Concorde.

Tourist trap
▼ **21st October,** *Athens*

Sgt R Gregory and driver A Hardman take time out to enjoy a tour of the Acropolis in Athens, a week after liberating the city.

Short-lived celebrations
▶ **September,** *Eindhoven, the Netherlands*

Scenes of jubilation in the streets as forces liberate the city of Eindhoven prove short-lived. Heavy German bombing later kills many civilians, the Allied forces are forced to withdraw and Operation Market Garden fails.

TIMELINE

17th September

Operation Market Garden: an audacious plan to end the war by Christmas is launched. Allied paratroops' attempts to capture key points to cross the river Rhine into Germany through the Netherlands fail when the objective of capturing Arnhem proves too ambitious.

14th October

Field Marshall Rommel takes his own life, rather than face trial over his involvement in a plot against Hitler.

20th October

US forces land in the Philippines, the latest success in a series of landings and attacks in the Pacific theatre, as the Americans continue to turn the tide of war against Japan. Some 60,000 troops land at Leyte, almost 30 months since they were forced to retreat.

Paper boys

21st July, *Chicago, USA*

Newspaper boys hold up the Chicago papers reporting the previous day's attempted assassination of Hitler by German Army officers. This was perhaps the most audacious of many attempts to assassinate the Führer.

1944

Battle of the Bulge
▲ **20th December, St Vith, Belgium**
M4 Sherman tanks take up their positions during the Ardennes campaign – the last major German offensive of the war.

Defensive positions
▶ **19th December, Ardennes, Belgium**
American troops man trenches along the snowy hedgerow during the battle of the Bulge, which costs the Americans around 19,000 lives.

1944

On patrol
◀ *St Vith, Belgium*
Soldiers of the US 7th Armored Division patrol St Vith, which is under attack by Wehrmacht forces. The town would be mostly destroyed in the battle of the Bulge.

Making a break
◀ *23rd December, Ardennes, Belgium*
American soldiers help fleeing locals to load themselves and some possession onto US trucks during a lull in the battle of the Bulge.

TIMELINE

23-26 October
Battle of Leyte Gulf, during which the Japanese make the first organised use of kamikaze aircraft.

20th November
With Soviet troops getting ever closer, Hitler leaves his Wolf's Lair headquarters and returns to Berlin.

16th December
Battle of the Bulge: hoping to drive a wedge between the advancing US and British forces in the area, Germany launches a massive offensive in the Ardennes forest. Within a few days, US troops are besieged at Bastogne in freezing conditions with inadequate supplies and ammunition. Around 19,000 US troops are killed before the offensive is defeated in late January.

Heads of state

9th February, *Yalta, Ukraine*

British Prime Minister Winston Churchill, US President Franklin D Roosevelt and Soviet Premier Joseph Stalin pose for photographs during their conference to discuss plans for post-war Europe.

1945

The final stages of the war revealed the horrific reality of what humanity is capable of. The war was over – but at what cost?

By the turn of the year, the Germans' final offensive against the Allies in the Ardennes was failing, and it seemed that, finally, it was only a matter of time until the Nazis capitulated. However, despite the inevitability of defeat, they continued to fight to the bitter end on all fronts. It wasn't until the spring that the deaths of Hitler and Mussolini presaged the Red Army taking Berlin, and the unconditional surrender that eventually brought the VE Day celebrations in May.

The celebrations were tempered, however, by the news filtering through of the indescribable scenes that greeted Allied troops entering Nazi concentration camps.

But the war was still not yet over. Fighting continued in Burma, while in the Pacific, General MacArthur's progress saw fierce and intense fighting with a Japanese resistance prepared to make the ultimate sacrifice for its country.

Ultimately, US President Harry S Truman felt he had no option but to deliver the first atomic bombs to the Japanese cities of Hiroshima and Nagasaki, with devastating effect. Finally, the Japanese surrender at the end of the summer brought the war to an end. **H**

Hands across the water
◀ *25th April, River Elbe, Germany*

Soviet and American (in helmets) troops drink each other's health when their forces meet at the Elbe river, south of Torgau, Germany.

TIMELINE

12th January
At Churchill's request, the Soviets bring forward the Vistula-Oder offensive to relieve pressure in the Ardennes.

17th January
A combined force of Soviet and Polish troops liberates the ruined city of Warsaw.

27th January
Soviet troops liberate Auschwitz, the largest of the Nazi concentration camps. Since 1942, around 1.2 millions Jews, Poles, Roma and Soviet POWs have been killed at the network of camps at Auschwitz.

4th February
Meeting at Yalta, Ukraine, of Allied leaders Churchill, Roosevelt and Stalin to discuss the occupation of Germany.

1945

Raising the flag
◄ **23rd February, Iwo Jima, the Bonin Islands**
This still from Marine photographer Bill Genaust's film captures the iconic moment of the raising of the Stars and Stripes at Iwo Jima.

On the beach
▶ **Saipan**
American soldiers fill sandbags on the beach at Saipan, in the Northern Mariana Islands. With the taking of Saipan, the Japanese home islands were now within striking distance of American B-29 superfortress bombers. The loss of the island forced the resignation of Prime Minister Hideki Tōjō.

TIMELINE

13-15th February
Allied bombing of Dresden, Germany, creates a firestorm over 1,000°C. Tens of thousands are killed.

19th February
Battle of Iwo Jima: the start of a month of some of the fiercest fighting in the Pacific theatre of the war.

9-10th March
Tokyo is the first Japanese city to be subjected to incendiary bombing, killing around 100,000 citizens.

1st April
US forces land on Okinawa, the beginning of months of intense fighting to secure the strategic island.

12th April
US President Franklin D Roosevelt dies from a stroke. Vice President Harry S Truman is sworn in as president.

1945

A helping hand
▼ 1945, *Okinawa*
American GIs escort a local woman away from the front lines during the battle of Okinawa.

Kamikaze pilots
▲ 1945
Japanese kamikaze pilots bow before their flights. Around 2,550 of these suicide missions were flown by June 1945 but with decreasing effectiveness.

Pigeon post
▲ 14th August, *Okinawa*
Sgt Herbert A Rollins tends to his carrier pigeons. Enemy troops would try to shoot down these important message-carriers.

15th April
The Bergen-Belsen concentration camp in Germany is liberated. Many inmates are beyond saving.

28th April
Benito Mussolini and his mistress Clara Petacci are executed by Italian partisans. Their bodies are dumped in a public square in Milan, where they are attacked. They are later hung from meat hooks and stoned.

30th April
Adolf Hitler and his new wife Eva Braun commit suicide in his bunker in Berlin. Their bodies are burned in the Chancellery garden, along with those of Joseph Goebbels and his wife and six children. Two days later, the Red Army takes Berlin.

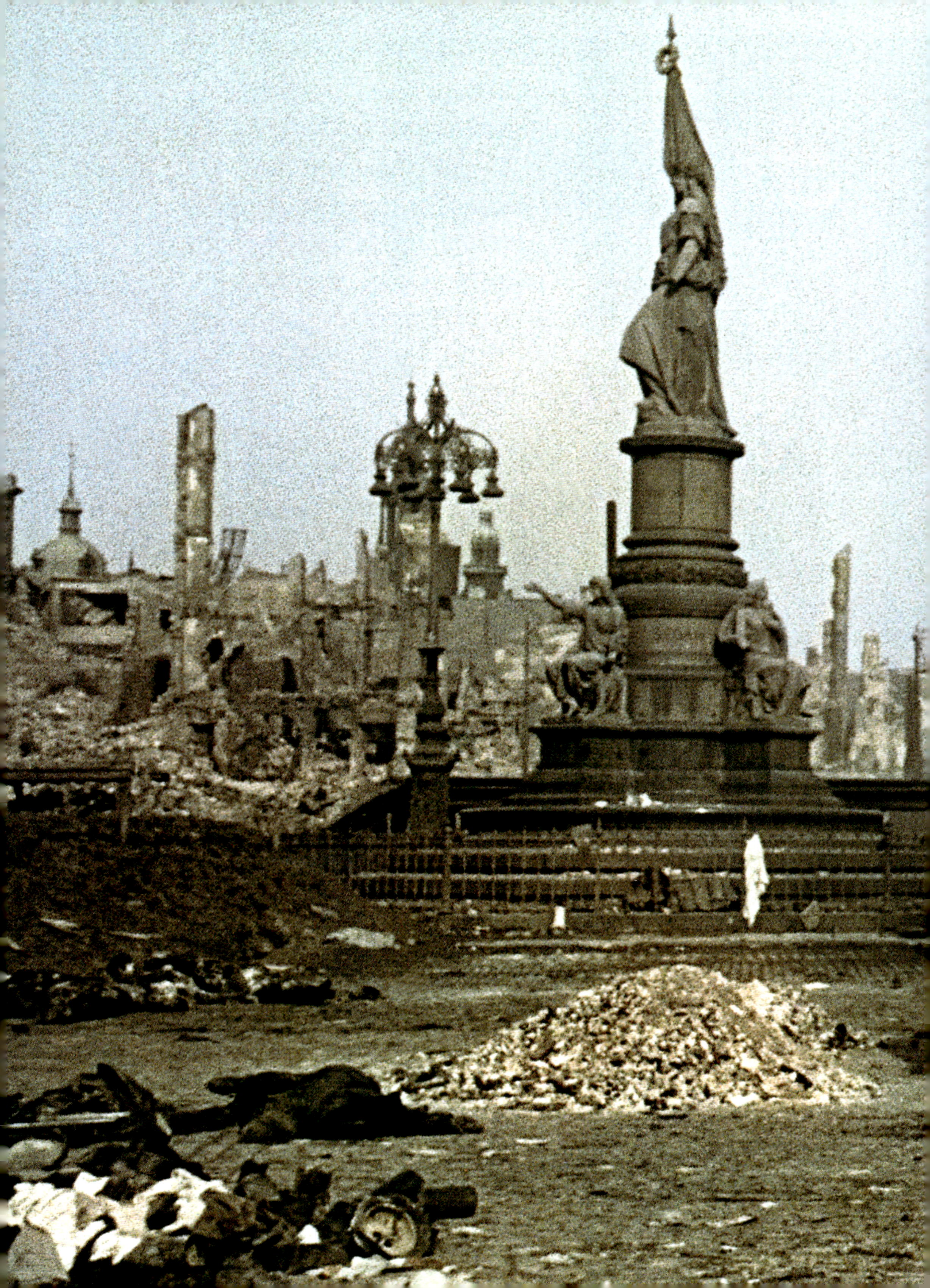

1945

Funeral pyre

25th February, *Dresden, Germany*
Bodies are piled and cremated at the Altmarkt near the Victory Monument in Dresden. The city had little or no anti-aircraft guns and lacked a civil defence system. The bombing has been the subject of much debate ever since, with many questioning the morality of such an attack, which left tens of thousands of civilians dead.

Free at last

April, *Buchenwald concentration camp, Germany*
Soldiers of the US 6th Armored Division talk to former prisoners about what had taken place at this, the largest concentration camp in Germany. After the war, the Soviets continued to use Buchenwald as an internment camp, with up to 10,000 prisoners dying there between 1945–1950.

1945

Poignant remains
▲ **April, *Buchenwald, Germany***

A former prisoner holds a human bone above a pile of bones from the camp's crematory. Around 65,000 people are believed to have died at Buchenwald, including Jews, Poles, Slovenes, homosexuals, political prisoners, POWs, the mentally ill and the physically disabled.

Emaciated survivors
▶ **April, *Dachau***

The oldest of the German concentration camps, Dachau was finally liberated on 29th April. In the weeks before, the Nazis attempts to evacuate the camp and remove all evidence led to thousands of deaths and an unsuccessful attempted camp coup.

Boy in the striped pyjamas
▲ **15th April, *Buchenwald, Germany***

A boy following the liberation. The Nazis had tried to evacuate the camp before the Allies could liberate it.

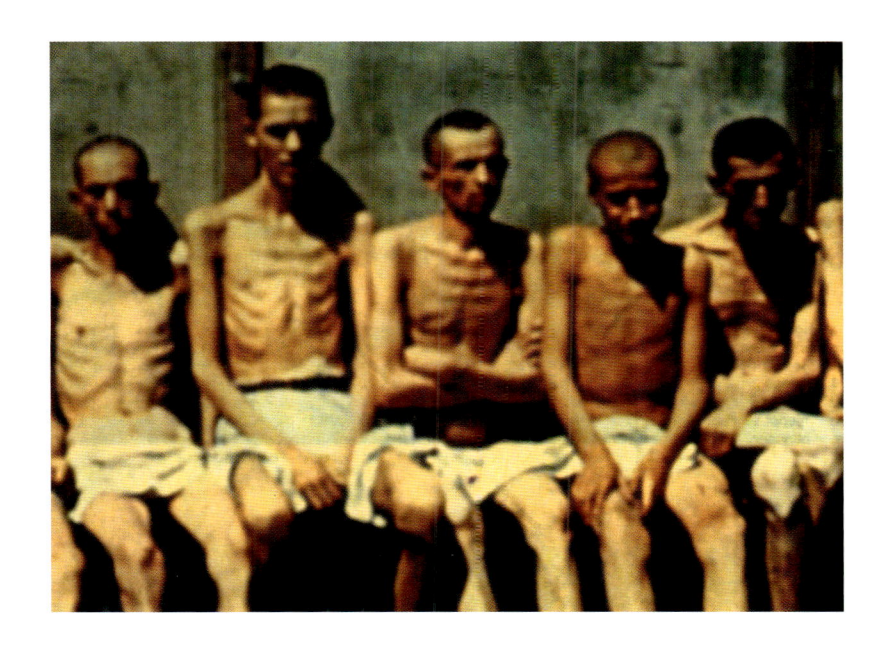

TIMELINE

7th May — At a formal ceremony in Reims, France, Germany surrenders unconditionally to the Allies.

8th May — Millions of people around Europe celebrate VE (Victory in Europe) Day.

6th June — The Allies effectively divide Germany into four zones - American, British, French and Soviet, as agreed at Yalta.

21st June — The US takes Okinawa. They have suffered up to 62,000 casualties in the campaign, many to kamikaze attacks.

16th July — The first atomic weapons test is conducted near Alamogordo, New Mexico, ahead of use against Japan.

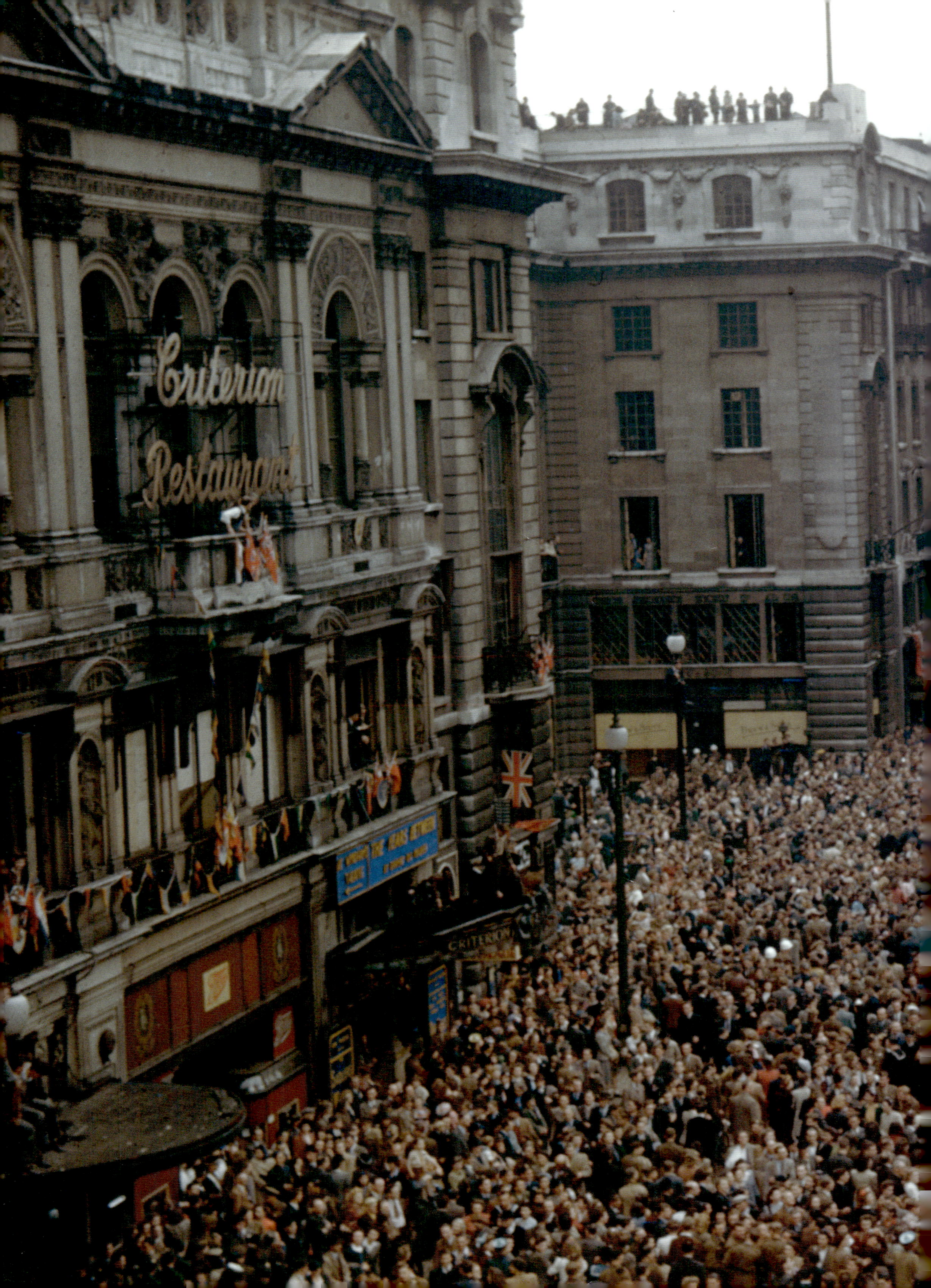
Criterion
Restaurant

1945

Victory in Europe

8th May, *Piccadilly Circus, London*

Vast crowds fill Piccadilly Circus to enjoy VE Day. Huge gatherings around the world celebrate victory in Europe. Princess Elizabeth, the future Queen Elizabeth II, and her sister Princess Margaret, wandered incognito among the crowds outside Buckingham Palace to taste the atmosphere. "I think it was one of the most memorable nights of my life," the Queen would later recall.

Nelson's Column

London
Trafalgar Square is decked with bunting and flags to celebrate the end of the war.

1945

The end is nigh
◀ **7th May,**
Reims, France
Colonel General Alfred Jodl signs the unconditional surrender on behalf of new German President Karl Dönitz.

Fly the flag
▶ **7th May,**
New York
Flag-sellers do brisk trade on the streets as New Yorkers come out in force to celebrate VE Day.

TIMELINE

17th July
The final Allied strategic conference of the war begins at Potsdam, near Berlin.

26th July
Clement Atlee defeats Winston Churchill by a landslide in the general election to become Britain's new Prime Minister. The Potsdam conference issues an ultimatum to Japan: unconditional surrender or face "prompt and utter destruction".

6th August
The world's first atomic bomb is detonated above Hiroshima. The burst-point immediately reaches temperatures 10,000 times hotter than the surface of the sun. US President Harry Truman calls it "the greatest thing in history".

BBC History Magazine 107

Atomic-bomb dome

Hiroshima, Japan
The ruins of the Hiroshima Prefectural Industrial Promotion Hall stand almost intact among the devastation. Today, the ruin forms part of the Hiroshima Peace Memorial Park.

1945

Vanished city
◀ **August, Hiroshima, Japan**
This USAF photograph shows the devastation of Hiroshima. The Hiroshima Peace Memorial Museum says that 140,000 were killed either directly or from radiation by the end of the year.

Soldiers return
▶ **5th October, Nagasaki, Japan**
Japanese soldiers survey bomb damage two months after the bomb that is thought to have killed 45,000 Japanese and brought to war to an end.

TIMELINE

8th August
The Soviet Union declares war on Japan.

9th August
A second atomic bomb is dropped, on Nagasaki. The city is selected as one of the few remaining intact.

15th August
Emperor Hirohito announces on radio that Japan is to surrender to the Allies.

2nd September
Japan formally surrenders to the Allies aboard the USS *Missouri*; the war is officially over. In total, as many as 66 million people are thought to have been killed in combat, through bombings, in POW or concentration camps, and through other atrocities since 1939.

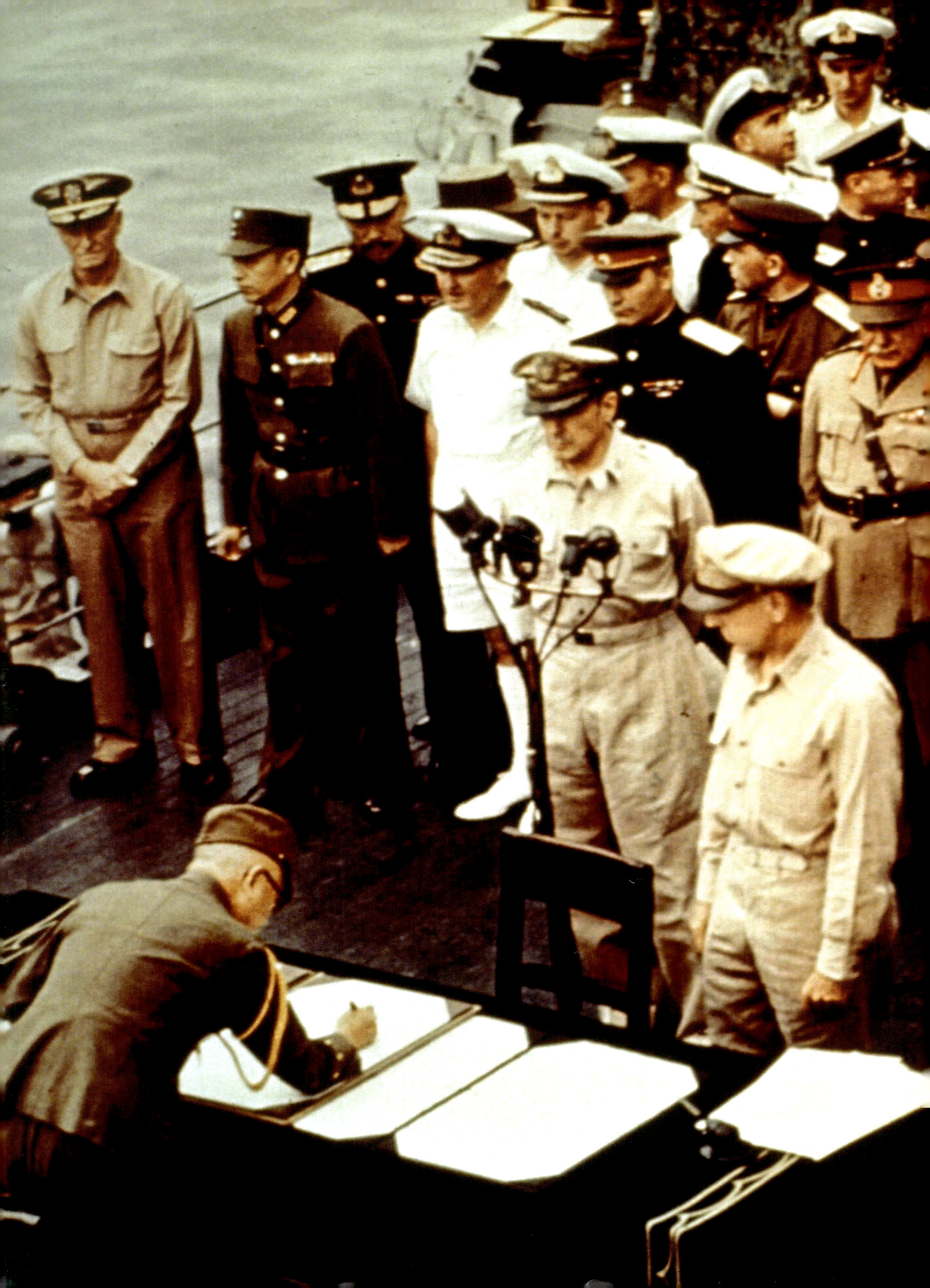

1945

War is over

2nd September, Tokyo
General Yoshijirō signs the instrument of surrender on behalf of the Japanese armed forces aboard the USS *Missouri* in Tokyo Bay, formally concluding the Second World War.

BBC HISTORY
SUBSCRIPTION ORDER FORM

BKZWW213

Please complete the order form and send to: **BBC History Magazine, FREEPOST LON 16059, Sittingbourne, Kent ME9 8DF**

UK DIRECT DEBIT
☐ I would like to subscribe by Direct Debit and **get my first 5 issues for £5***. After this my subscription will continue at £19 every 6 issues by Direct Debit – **still saving 25%** [please complete the form below]

YOUR DETAILS (ESSENTIAL)
Title _____ Forename _____
Surname _____
Address _____
_____
_____ Postcode _____
Home phone no _____
Mobile tel no** _____
Email** _____

☐ **I wish to purchase a gift subscription** (please supply gift recipient's name and address on a separate sheet)

Instructions to your Bank or Building Society to pay by Direct Debit — Direct Debit

To: the Manager (Bank/Building Society) _____
Address _____
_____ Postcode _____
Name(s) of account holder(s) _____
Bank/Building Society account number ☐☐☐☐☐☐☐☐
Branch sort code ☐☐ ☐☐ ☐☐
Reference number (internal use only) ☐☐☐☐☐☐☐☐☐☐

Originator's identification number: **7 1 0 6 4 4**

Please pay Immediate Media Co Bristol Ltd Debits from the account detailed in this instruction subject to the safeguards assured by the Direct Debit Guarantee. I understand that this instruction may remain with Immediate Media Co Bristol Ltd and, if so, details will be passed electronically to my Bank / Building Society.

Signature _____ Date __/__/__

Banks and Building Societies may not accept Direct Debit mandates from some types of account.

Immediate Media Company Limited (publishers of *BBC History Magazine* under licence from BBC Worldwide) would love to keep you informed by post or telephone of special offers and promotions from the Immediate Media Company Group. Please tick if you'd prefer not to receive these ☐
** Please enter this information so that *BBC History Magazine* may keep you informed of newsletters, special offers and other promotions by email or text message. You may unsubscribe from these at any time. Please tick here if you'd like to receive details of special offers from BBC Worldwide via email ☐

OTHER PAYMENT METHODS
☐ **UK Cheque/Credit/Debit card** – just £41.45 for 13 issues – **save 25%**
☐ **Europe inc Eire** – £56.25 for 13 issues
☐ **Rest of World** – £58 for 13 issues
☐ I enclose a cheque made payable to Immediate Media Co Ltd. for £ _____

☐ Visa ☐ Mastercard ☐ Maestro
☐☐☐☐ ☐☐☐☐ ☐☐☐☐ ☐☐☐☐

Issue no. ☐☐ Valid from ☐☐☐☐ Expiry date ☐☐☐☐

Signature _____ Date _____

OVERSEAS Please complete the order form and send to: *BBC History Magazine*, PO Box 279, Sittingbourne, Kent ME9 8DF

*5 issues for £5 offer only available to UK Direct Debit orders. After this your subscription will continue at £19 every 6 issues by Direct Debit. If you cancel within 2 weeks of receiving your 4th issue, you will pay no more than £5. Your subscription will start with the next available issue. **Offer ends 31 December 2013.**

You may photocopy this form

Try a subscription to Britain's bestselling history magazine

Don't miss out – subscribe today...

- Try your first **5 issues for just £5***
- Continue to **save 25%** at just **£19 every 6 issues** by Direct Debit thereafter
- **Free UK delivery** direct to your door
- Don't miss any of the amazing content in the **UK's bestselling history magazine**
- **Hurry!** Offer ends 31 December 2013

5 issues for £5*

when you try a subscription to *BBC History Magazine*

---

3 WAYS TO ORDER

ONLINE
www.buysubscriptions.com/historymagazine

PLEASE QUOTE BKZWW213

BY PHONE
0844 844 0250+

PLEASE QUOTE BKZWW213

BY POST
BBC History Magazine,
FREEPOST LON 16059,
Sittingbourne,
Kent, ME9 8DF

+ Calls to this number from a BT landline will cost no more than 5p per minute. Calls from mobiles and other providers may vary. Lines are open 8am-8pm weekdays & 9am-1pm Saturday.

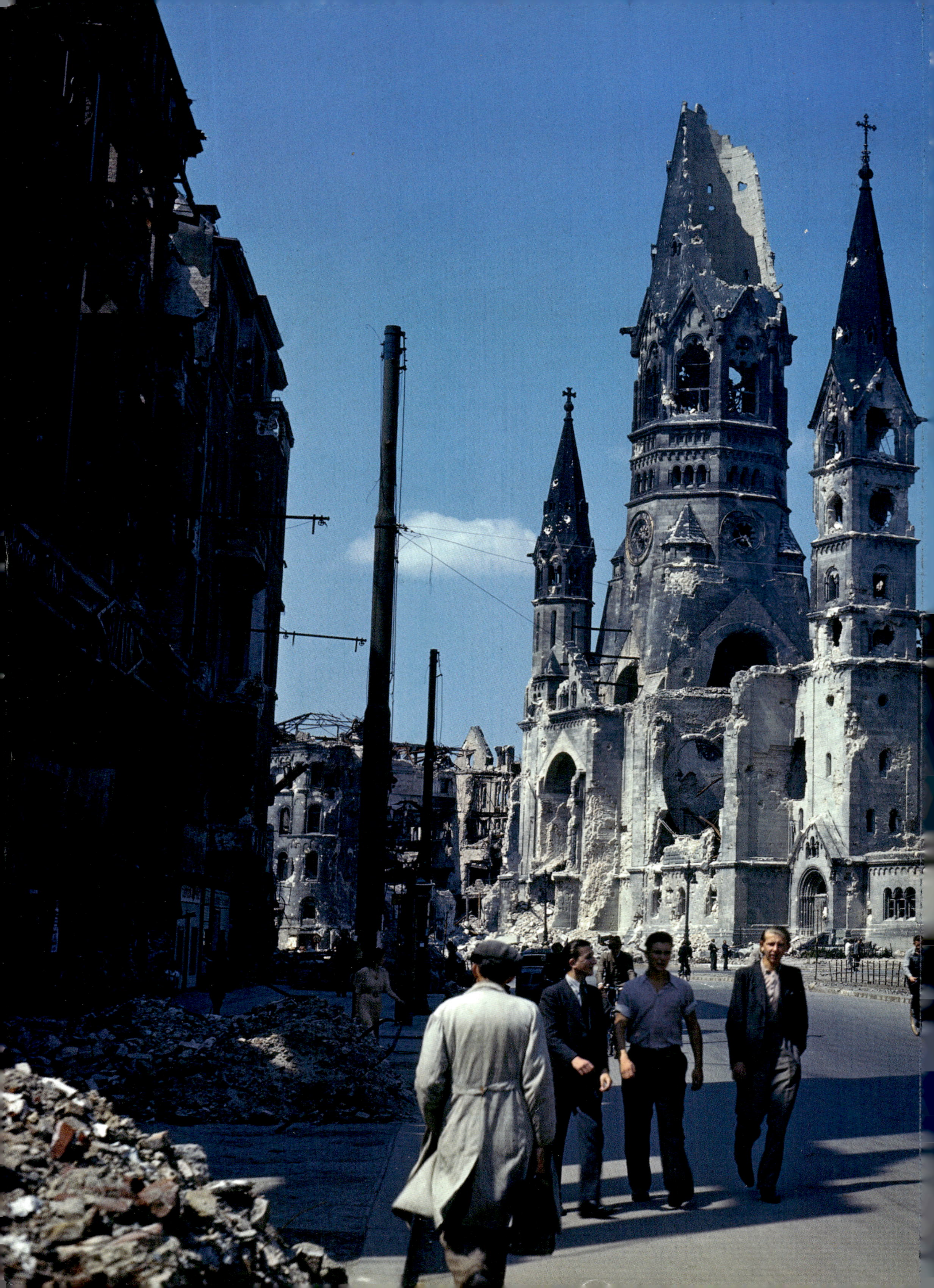

Traditional Aran Island Knitting

Pam Dawson

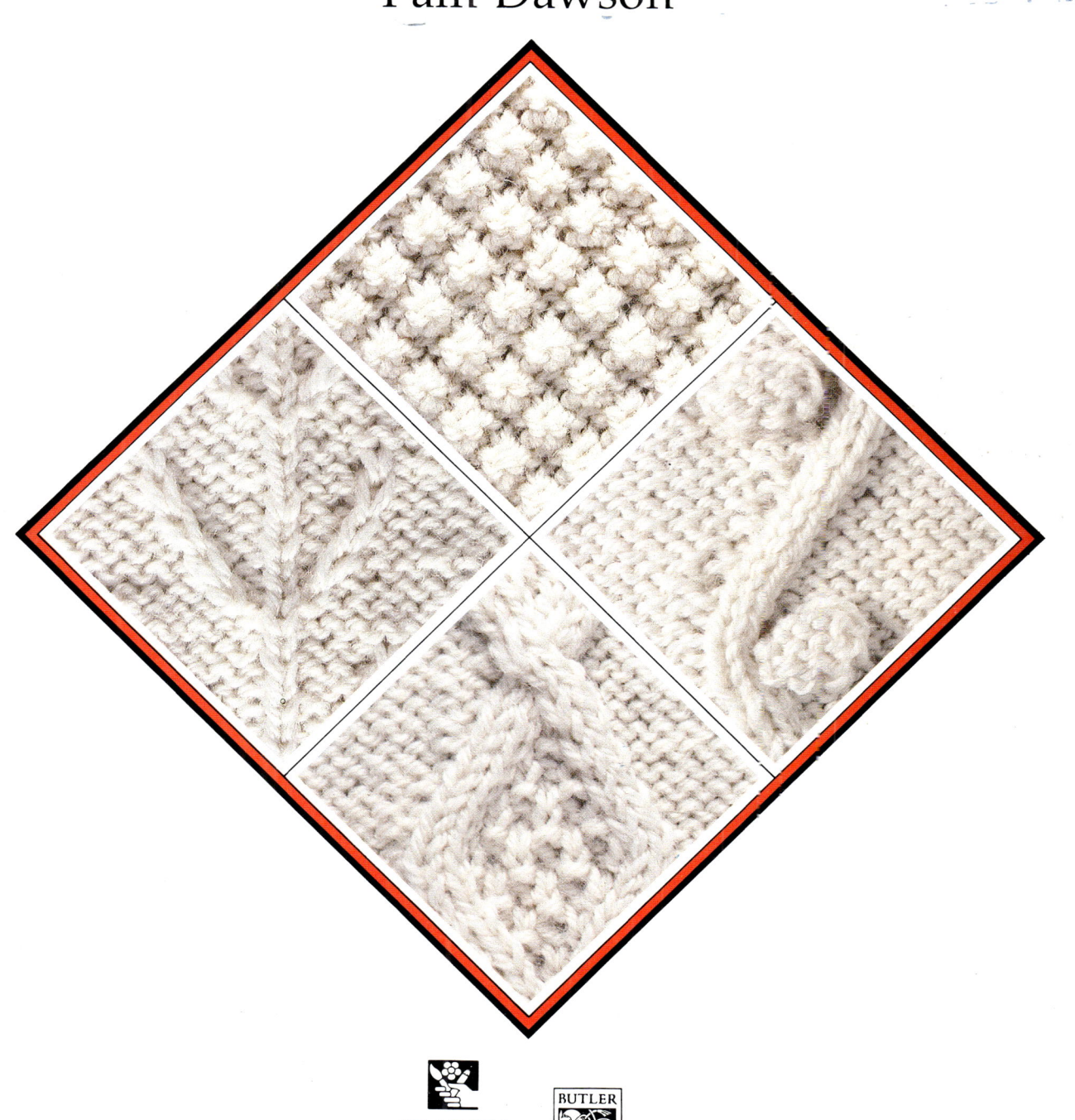

SEARCH PRESS

BUTLER SIMS

First published in Great Britain 1991
Search Press Limited
Wellwood, North Farm Road,
Tunbridge Wells, Kent TN2 3DR
in association with
Butler Sims Ltd,
55 Merrion Square,
Dublin 2, Ireland

Copyright © Search Press Ltd 1991

Photography by Search Press Studios

The publishers acknowledge with thanks permission to reproduce the photograph and engraving shown in this book: Ralph Kleinhempel GmbH & Co for the *Knitting Madonna*, page 3, and The National Museum of Ireland, Dublin, for the spinning wheel from Belleek, Co. Fermanagh, page 7.

All rights reserved. No part of this book may be reproduced in any form, by print, photoprint, microfilm, microfiche, mechanical recording, photocopying, translation, or by any means, known or as yet unknown, or stored in an information retrieval system, without written permission obtained beforehand from Search Press Limited. The illustrations are strictly copyright and may not be copied for commercial purposes without the permission of Search Press Limited, to whom all enquiries in connection with this book, or any part of it, should be addressed.

ISBN 0 85532 688 3 (UK)
     0 946049 05 X (Ireland)

SPINNERS ADDRESSES

Jaeger yarns (UK)
Jaeger Handknitting Ltd., McMullen Road, Darlington, Co. Durham, DL1 1YD.

AUSTRALIA
All enquiries to:
Coats Paton Handknitting, Thistle Street, Launceston 7250, Tasmania.

NEW ZEALAND
Coats Patons (New Zealand) Ltd., 263, Ti Rakan Drive, Pakuranga, Auckland.

USA
Susan Bates Inc., 212, Middlesex Avenue, Chester, CT 06412.

Robin yarns (UK)
Robin Wools Ltd., Robin Mills, Idle, Bradford, West Yorkshire, BD10 9TE.

AUSTRALIA
Karingal Vic/Tas Pty Ltd., 6, Macro Court, Rowville, Victoria 3178

CANADA
S.R. Kertzer Ltd., 105A Winges Road, Woodbridge, Toronto, Ontario L4L 6C2.

SOUTH AFRICA
Brasch Hobby, P.O. Box 6405, Johannesberg 2000.

USA
The Plymouth Yarn Co., P.O. Box 28, 500, Lafayette Street, Bristol, PA 19007.

Sunbeam yarns (UK)
Sunbeam Knitting Wools, Crawshaw Mills, Pudsey, Leeds, West Yorkshire, LS28 7BS.

USA
Tahki Imports, 11, Graphic Place, Moonachie, New Jersey 07074.

Photoset by Scribe Design, Gillingham, Kent
Printed in Spain by Elkar S. Coop, Bilbao 12

The Buxtehude altar piece, popularly called 'The Knitting Madonna' was painted by Meister Bertram of Minden, Germany, circa 1400 The Virgin Mary is shown using a set of four needles to knit the stitches around the neck of a garment.

Introduction

The craft of knitting has evolved over very many centuries and although it is impossible to say exactly where, and when it began, small fragments of interlocked fabric discovered during various periods of archaeological excavation seem to indicate that some form of knitting originated in Arabia. The nomad people of these regions did much to encourage the development of the craft and, quite early in its history, had produced a knitting frame very similar to the knitting bobbin used by children today.

From Arabia, different aspects of the craft eventually spread throughout the known world. In the early eighth century the Arabs began a policy of territorial expansion and gained control of part of the Iberian Peninsula. By the eleventh century, Spain had become the centre of the technique of knitting with needles, which we know today as hand-knitting. Knowledge of the craft spread rapidly to the rest of Europe and as knitting was closely linked with religion during this time, many of the finest examples were intended as church vestments and furnishings, see previous page.

No-one can be certain when knitting first appeared in Britain but, once introduced, it quickly became established and poverty-stricken families were quick to grasp the opportunity of earning an income in their own homes. By the thirteenth century the woollen industry, including the hand-spinning and dyeing of yarn, the weaving of cloth and knitting, had become one of the most profitable in our entire history. This trade was so important that many of the laws and customs of our country were established during this period to protect it—the first introduction of an export tax on the profitable commodity; a system of patrolling the seas with convoys of ships to overcome the problem of piracy and the use of a sack of wool as part of our parliamentary regalia, to remind all members of the source of the wealth of the country.

By the late fifteenth century, knitting had become associated with fashionable wearing apparel and such items as stockings, gloves, caps and shirts were produced in vast quantities. Examples of felted woollen caps of the early Tudor period are to be seen in the Victoria and Albert Museum in London and an Act of Parliament passed during the reign of Henry VII in 1488 relates to knitted caps. Glimpses of the general interest in knitting also appear casually in household accounts of the time, and it is obvious that the craft had been absorbed into the routine of everyday life.

It was not until the dawning of the Elizabethan age, however, that knitting became not just a practical, everyday craft but a creative and beautiful art form. The foundation of Knitting Guilds during this period brought together, for the first time, the colour appreciation and creative talent of the artist with the technical skill of the artisan. Men had always dominated the craft and although women and children had by now mastered the skill to add to meagre incomes, and schools had even been established to teach knitting, only men and boys were admitted to the Guilds. For a period of about six years an apprentice learned the various techniques, both at home and abroad, and his subsequent examination entailed knitting a shirt, a cap, a pair of stockings and a carpet, or wall-hanging.

During the reign of Elizabeth I, hand-knitted silk stockings became the vogue and it was during this period that the Reverend William Lee invented the first knitting frame capable of producing machine-made stockings. As these quickly replaced the coarser hand-knitted versions, the hosiery trade in and around London was formed. William Lee died in France some time after 1611, before realizing the profound influence his invention would eventually have on the knitting industry. The ancient craft of knitting can thus lay claim to being the forerunner of modern technology, long before the start of the industrial revolution.

With the advent of machine-knitting the old skills declined in most areas but the seventeenth and eighteenth centuries found them firmly established among the famous hand-knitters of the Yorkshire dales. Men, women and children knitted, singing special songs as they clicked away—the faster the rhythm the quicker they knitted. The invaluable knowledge of that period was never written down, but was passed from one generation to another by word of mouth. The craft barely survived during the nineteenth century, but a succession of wars requiring socks and Balaclava helmets for the troops, and the introduction of the popular 'cardigan' by the Earl of Cardigan, brought industry and some small profit to the inventive knitters of the dales.

During the comparatively peaceful times of the middle 1830s the first women's magazines appeared and these were to revolutionize the hand-knitting industry. Knitting soon gained enormous popularity, not as a necessary means of survival but as an interesting and therapeutic hobby. The oldest book in my library, entitled 'The Ladies' Knitting and Netting Book', First Series, is dated 1839. It is a fourth edition, which gives some indication as to its total sales. By modern standards it is crude; unillustrated, and with scant guidance about yarn, needle size and tension. A later book, 'The Lady's Knitting Book', first published in 1884, is also unillustrated and brief headings give little indication of the type of garment which will be produced. On one page a previous owner has found and corrected in ink an error in the instructions for knitting 'Spider stitch'—so mistakes due to human error happened even then!

Today we take full-colour illustrations of superb designs, row-by-row instructions, exact details of qualities and quantities, and correct tension for granted. It is also doubtful whether anything new can now be added to the wealth of technical knowledge, or the variety of stitches and complexities of patterns available to the avid hand-knitter. What does emerge from this welter of information is that however much fashions may come and go, traditional garments remain consistently popular. Rib patterns, cable variations, three-dimensional textures such as bobbles and coloured techniques all exist in knitting traditions throughout the world. What gives a distinctly regional influence to these techniques, however, is the way in which they have been combined in the past, and the type of yarn which has been used to produce different fabrics. Rib and cable patterns have become synonymous with fishermen's garments in almost every fishing port around the entire coastline of the British Isles. The traditional guernsey has a dropped shoulder-line and square armholes and is knitted in flat, brocade-like patterns. The more complex, three-dimensional texture of authentic Aran patterns produces garments which are instantly recognizable. The coloured patterns of the Shetland Isles, particularly Fair Isle, have been adapted as far afield as Iceland and the Falkland Isles. Shetland also continues to produce gossamer lace knitting of exquisite beauty and the traditional wedding ring shawl is unique.

Pam Dawson

Aran knitting

The mainland of Ireland is divided into four provinces. Northern Ireland is in the province of Ulster and is made up of six of Ulster's nine counties. The Republic of Ireland includes Leinster in the east which is divided into twelve counties, Munster in the south which has six counties, and to the east lies Connacht with five counties, including Galway.

The west coast of Ireland faces into the bleak Atlantic and some thirty miles out into Galway Bay lie the three islands of Aran. The largest of these is Inishmore, then comes Inishmaan and the smallest is Inisheer. The terrain of all three islands is rugged and barren and life has always been hard for the inhabitants. For centuries the islanders cultivated the sparse covering of soil overlaying the hard rock surface, using seaweed to manure their crops and to provide fodder for their sturdy sheep and cattle.

The everyday language of the inhabitants is Gaelic and local songs and stories tell of the folklore and culture of the islands and the mainland. The women of Ireland have always spun their own wool and woven tweed for clothing but it is a frustrating exercise trying to trace the history of knitting because there are so few written records, or actual early examples. Early references to the life and traditions of the islanders mention that men often wore a woollen sweater under a waistcoat. This is described as grey or blue in colour and not the creamy-white we know today.

The most distinctive features of Aran knitting are the heavily-embossed fabrics and intricate patterns. It is claimed that this type of knitting has been known in the islands for many centuries but it was most likely based on Austrian and central European techniques, which would not have developed until quite a late date in the history of Aran knitting. Another early source of inspiration for these twisted, interlocked and encrusted patterns is said to be The Book of Kells but this seems most improbable, as this wonderfully illuminated manuscript of the Gospels of Matthew, Mark, Luke and John, believed to have been written between the sixth and eighth centuries, is one of Ireland's greatest treasures. It would only have been accessible to a very few privileged churchmen and it is unlikely that the inhabitants of the remote Aran islands would have had an opportunity of seeing the original manuscript. It is far more likely that the ancient Celtic crosses to be found all over the mainland of Ireland and the Aran islands were the original source of design for these highly-textured patterns.

The first real growth of the Aran knitting industry would probably have been as a direct result of the disastrous potato famines in Ireland in the mid and late nineteenth century. Government programmes encouraged all types of cottage industries in an endeavour to alleviate the appalling poverty and suffering, and knitting and crochet were developed throughout Ireland to provide a source of income. The women of Aran proved to be most adept at knitting, while the women of the mainland perfected the many forms of crochet we still practice today.

Aran knitting yarn also played its part in the character of Aran knitting, as the wool was spun and dyed locally. Mosses and seaweed gave soft, muted colours and the differences in each fleece gave a wide range of natural colours, through browns and greys to cream. The traditional name for Aran wool is 'bainin', pronounced 'bawneen', and this is the Irish word for undyed wool. It describes not so much the texture of the wool as the shade and today we regard cream as the authentic colour and it is the most popular choice for all types of Aran garments.

The stitch patterns in all folk knitting are often inspired by things in common to each area, such as local flora and fauna and the events in daily working life. Aran designs use many patterns featured in fishermen's ganseys and guernseys, but these have taken on local meanings. The shape of the traditional sweaters are classical and the whole emphasis is placed on the texture of the fabric, which had to be wind and weatherproof to withstand the often inhospitable climate.

The harsh and unspoilt way of life in the islands has altered dramatically in the past few decades, largely as a result of a thriving tourist industry and a planned revival of interest in the cottage crafts. Aran knitting has been particularly important in raising the standard of living and today there is a world-wide demand for these popular garments. We will never be able to trace the past history of the craft, but it is true to say that The Book of Kells and Celtic crosses have influenced Aran patterns in modern times and will probably continue to be a marvellous source of inspiration for these unique examples of hand-knitting in the future.

This book contains details of the techniques used in some of the stitch patterns featured in Aran designs, together with row-by-row instructions for some traditional examples. The garments which follow have been designed to highlight authentic features, while still being practical for today's life-style.

*The women of Ireland have always spun their own wool.
This multiple spinning wheel from Belleek, Co. Fermanagh, circa 1818,
was designed to allow four spinners to work simultaneously.*

Bobble patterns

Small, raised areas of knitting, which stand proud from the surface, are termed bobbles. These stitches are used extensively in Aran knitting and do much to give the fabric its characteristic three-dimensional appearance.

To work bobble stitches

The bobbles can be varied in size and in their position on the background fabric.

To make a small purl bobble against a stocking stitch background, work until the position for the bobble is reached. K1, P1, K1 all into the next stitch making three stitches out of one. Turn the needle, leaving the rest of the row unworked and knit these three stitches, then turn the needle again and purl three. To complete the bobble, use the point of the left hand needle to lift the second and third stitches over the top of the first stitch and off the needle, leaving the original stitch, (see Fig 1).

To make a large knit bobble against a reversed stocking stitch background, work until the position for the bobble is reached. Knit into the front and back of the next stitch twice, then into the front again, making five stitches out of one. Turn the needle, leaving the rest of the row unworked and purl these five stitches, then turn the needle again and knit five, then repeat these two rows so that you have worked the stitches four times. To complete the bobble, use the point of the left hand needle to lift the second, third, fourth and fifth stitches over the top of the first stitch and off the needle, leaving the original stitch, (see Fig 2).

fig 2 completing a large bobble

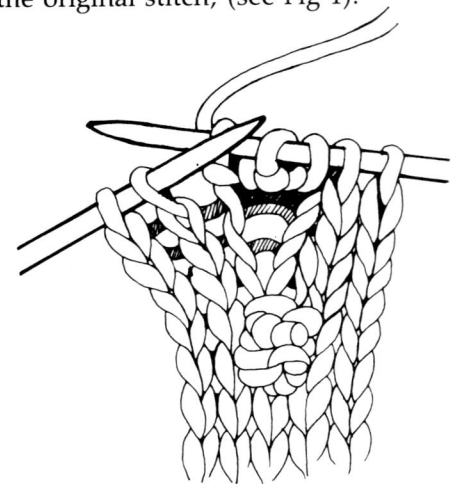

fig 1 completing a small bobble

Helping hand

When knitting a garment in a chunky weight, such as an Aran quality, seaming may be a problem. As a guide-line do not use a yarn thicker than a Double Knitting weight for seaming. If the knitting yarn is thicker, use a finer colour match.

The one area where neat seaming is essential is on the shoulder-line. The stepped effect of normal casting off in blocks of stitches is difficult to disguise. The following method gives a neat finish to all garments.

On a left front shoulder edge, or right back shoulder edge, when the point has been reached for the shoulder shaping, instead of casting off the required number of stitches at the beginning of the next knit row, on the *previous* purl row work to within this number of stitches, then turn the work. Slip the first stitch on the left hand needle then knit to the end of the row. Repeat this for the required number of rows, then purl across all the stitches on the last row. Cast off on the next knit row in the usual way, (see Fig 3).

On a right front shoulder edge, or left back shoulder edge, work as given above but reverse the shaping by beginning on a *knit* row.

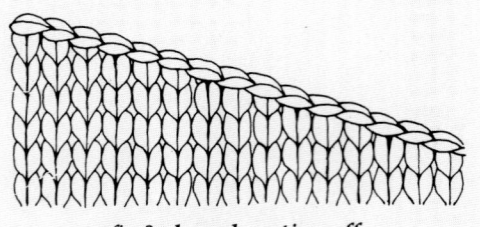

fig 3 shaped casting off

Traditional Aran patterns

Bobbles, cables and travelling stitches all play their part in the intricate patterns used in Aran knitting, and many of them have been given local names.

Trinity pattern

This simple stitch is also called blackberry pattern and its name derives from the method of working three stitches into one, and one stitch into three. It requires multiples of 4 stitches, plus 3, eg 19.
1st row (Rs) P to end.
2nd row K1, *(K1, P1, K1) into the next stitch, P3 tog, rep from * to the last 2 sts, (K1, P1, K1) into the next stitch, K1. Note that extra stitches have been increased in this row.
3rd row P to end.
4th row K1, *P3 tog, (K1, P1, K1) into the next stitch, rep from * to the last 4 sts, P3 tog, K1. Note that the stitches have now reverted to their original number.
These 4 rows form the pattern.

Diamond panel

In this pattern two lines of travelling stitches worked in opposite directions are combined to form the diamond shape. The centre of each diamond is filled in with Irish moss stitch, a variation of single moss stitch worked over two rows instead of one. This sample has been worked as a panel over 14 stitches.
1st row (Rs) P5, K4, P5.
2nd and every foll alt row K all P sts of previous row and P all K sts; thus, this row will read K5, P4, K5.
3rd row P5, sl next 2 sts on to cable needle and hold at front of work, K2 from left hand needle then K2 from cable needle — called C4F —, P5.
5th row P4, sl next st on to cable needle and hold at back of work, K2 from left hand needle then K1 from cable needle — called Cr2R —, sl next 2 sts on to cable needle and hold at front of work, P1 from left hand needle then K2 from cable needle — called Cr2L —, P4.
7th row P3, Cr2R, P1, K1, Cr2L, P3.
9th row P2, Cr2R, (P1, K1) twice, Cr2L, P2.
11th row P1, Cr2R, (P1, K1) 3 times, Cr2L, P1.
13th row P1, Cr2L, (K1, P1) 3 times, Cr2R but work P1 from cable needle instead of K1, P1.
15th row P2, Cr2L, (K1, P1) twice, Cr2R as 13th row, P2.
17th row P3, Cr2L, K1, P1, Cr2R as 13th row, P3.
19th row P4, Cr2L, Cr2R as 13th row, P4.
20th row As 2nd row.
The 3rd to 20th rows form the pattern.

Zigzag and bobble panel

In this pattern two stitches travel across the fabric to form a zigzag line, with bobbles placed on either side of the zigzag. This sample has been worked as a panel over 14 stitches.

1st row (Rs) P3, K2, P9.
2nd and every foll alt row K all P sts of previous row and P all K sts: thus, this row will read K9, P2, K3.
3rd row P3, sl next 2 sts on to cable needle and hold at front of work, P1 from left hand needle then K2 from cable needle — called Cr2L —, P8.
5th row P4, Cr2L, P7.
7th row P5, Cr2L, P6.
9th row P6, Cr2L, P5.
11th row P7, Cr2L, P4.
13th row P5, (K into front and back of next st) twice then K into front again, (turn and K5, turn and P5) twice, use left hand needle to lift 2nd, 3rd, 4th and 5th sts over first st and off needle — called B1 —, P2, Cr2L, P3.
15th row P8, sl next st on to cable needle and hold at back of work, K2 from left hand needle then P1 from cable needle — called Cr2R —, P3.
17th row P7, Cr2R, P4.
19th row P6, Cr2R, P5.
21st row P5, Cr2R, P6.
23rd row P4, Cr2R, P7.
25th row P3, Cr2R, P2, B1, P5.
26th row As 2nd row.
The 3rd to 26th rows form the pattern.

Tree of life pattern

Single lines of travelling stitches branch out from the central stitch to form this traditional pattern. To work as an all-over fabric this sample requires multiples of 15 stitches, or it can be worked as a single panel over 15 stitches.

1st row (Rs) *P7, K1, P7, rep from * in this and subsequent rows to form an all-over fabric.
2nd row *K7, P1, K7.
3rd row *P5, sl next st on to cable needle and hold at back of work, K1 from left hand needle then P1 from cable needle — called C2B —, K1 from left hand needle, sl next st on to cable needle and hold at front of work, P1 from left hand needle then K1 from cable needle — called C2F —, P5.
4th row *K5, sl 1 in a P-wise direction keeping yarn at front of work, K1, P1, K1, sl 1, K5.
5th row *P4, C2B, P1, K1, P1, C2F, P4.
6th row *K4, sl 1, K2, P1, K2, sl 1, K4.
7th row *P3, C2B, P2, K1, P2, C2F, P3.
8th row *K3, sl 1, K3, P1, K3, sl 1, K3.
9th row *P2, C2B, P3, K1, P3, C2F, P2.
10th row *K2, sl 1, K4, P1, K4, sl 1, K2.
These 10 rows form the pattern.

Opposite: Traditional Aran patterns have been incorporated into this design but the stitches are enhanced by the use of an Aran tweed yarn, (see pattern on page 13).
Designed by Pat Menchini.

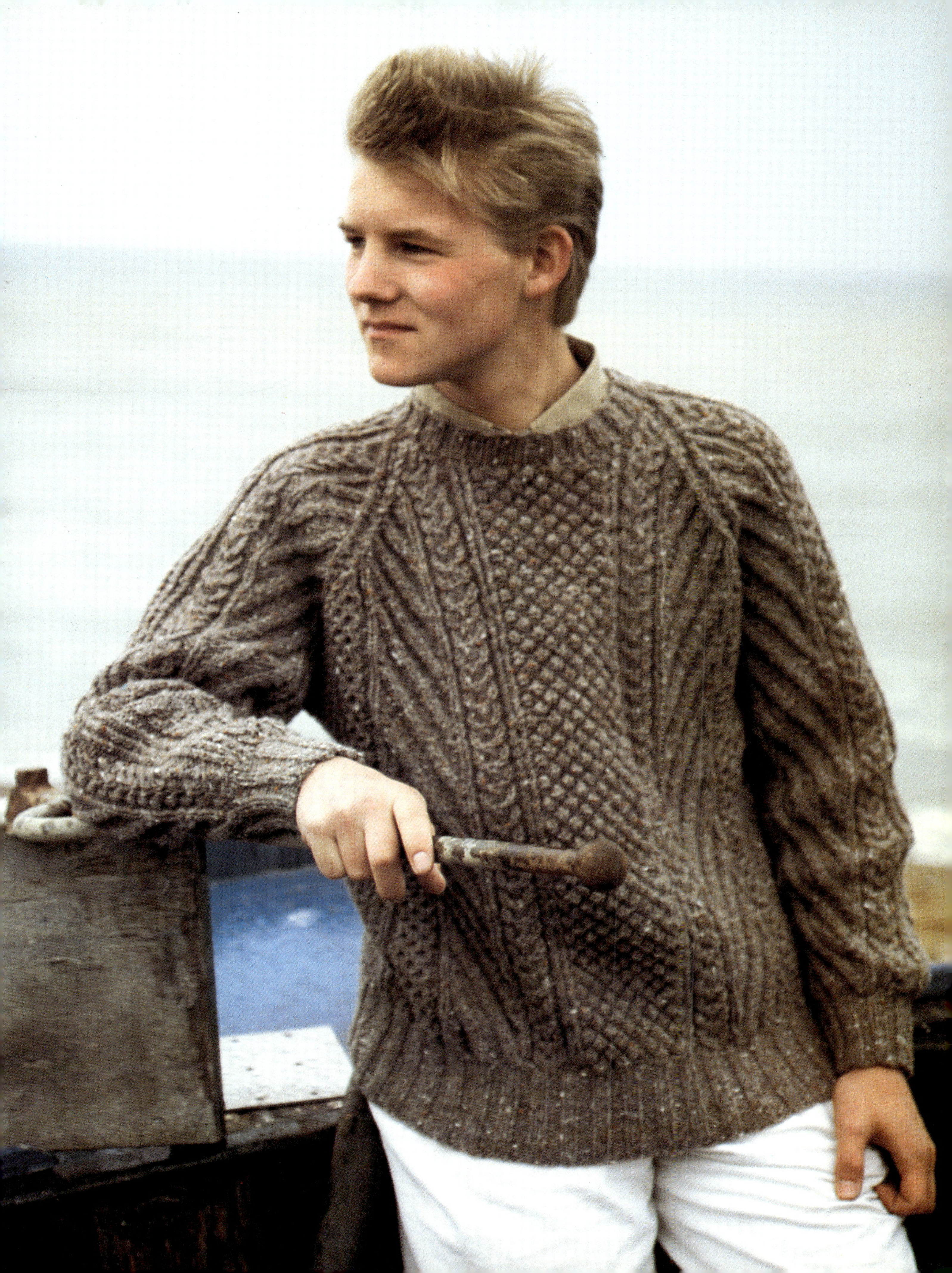

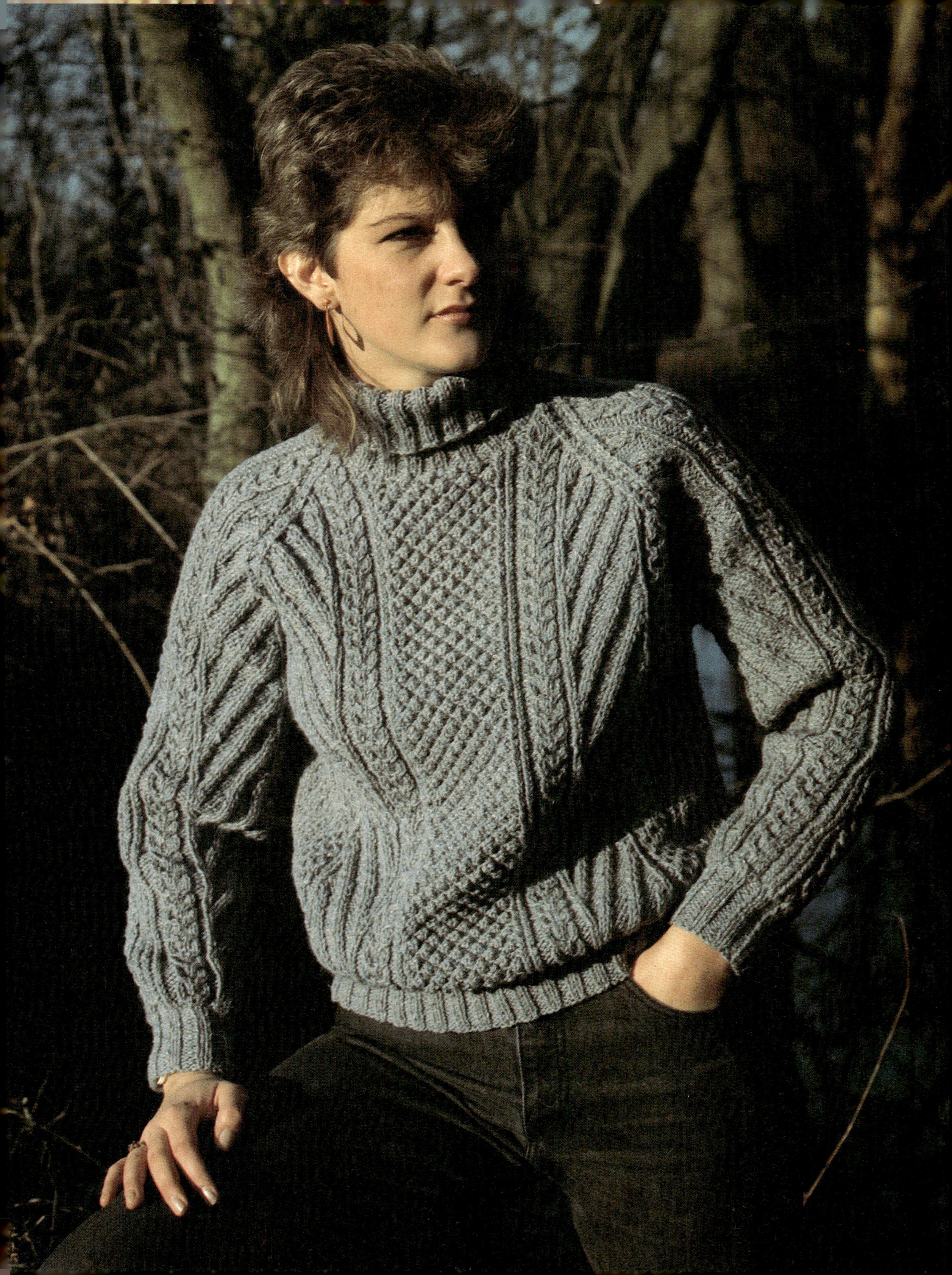

Aran jersey with raglan sleeves

This design features traditional stitch patterns, such as Trinity stitch and honeycomb and is suitable for a man or a woman. The raglan sleeves make for ease-of-movement and the garment can be completed with a neat crew neck, or a snug polo collar.

Measurements
To fit 36[38:40:42]in/ 91[97:102:107]cm bust/chest
Actual measurements, 42[44:46:48]in/107[112:117:122]cm
Length to centre back neck, excluding neckband, 25½[26:26½:27]in/65[66:67:69]cm
Sleeve seam, 17[18:18½:18½]in/ 43[46:47:47]cm
The figures in [] refer to the 38/97, 40/102 and 42in/107cm sizes respectively

Materials
Round neck version, 21[21:22:22] × 50g balls of Sunbeam Aran Tweed
Polo neck version, 22[23:23:24] × 50g balls of same
One pair No 8/4mm needles
One pair No 6/5mm needles
Set of four No 8/4mm needles pointed at both ends
Cable needle
The quantities of yarn given are based on average requirements and are approximate

Tension
18 sts and 24 rows to 4in/10cm over st st worked on No 6/5mm needles

Opposite: The woman's version of the jersey shown on page 11 has a polo collar but you can work the round neckline if preferred. This jersey has raglan sleeves for ease of movement.
Designed by Pat Menchini.

Left panel pattern
Worked over 17 sts.
1st row (Rs) K1, (sl next st on to cable needle and hold at back of work, K2 from left hand needle then P1 from cable needle — abbreviated as C1BP —, P3) twice, C1BP, K1.
2nd and every foll alt row Work across 17 sts K all K sts and P all P sts, noting that this row will read P1, (K1, P2, K3) twice, K1, P2, P1.
3rd row K1, sl next st on to cable needle and hold at back of work, K1 then P1 from cable needle, (P3, C1BP) twice, P1, K1.
5th row K1, P4, C1BP, P3, C1BP, P2, K1.
7th row K1, (P3, C1BP) twice, P3, K1.
9th row K1, P2, (C1BP, P3) twice, K2.
11th row K1, P1, (C1BP, P3) twice, sl next st on to cable needle and hold at back of work, K1 from left hand needle then K1 from cable needle — abbreviated as CB—, K1.
12th row As 2nd row.
These 12 rows form left panel.

Right panel pattern
Worked over 17 sts.
1st row (Rs) K1, (sl next 2 sts on to cable needle and hold at front of work, P1 from left hand needle then K2 from cable needle — abbreviated as C2FP —, P3) twice, C2FP, K1.
2nd and every foll alt row As 2nd row of left panel, noting that this row will read P1, (P2, K4) twice, P2, K1, P1.
3rd row K1, P1, (C2FP, P3) twice, sl next st on to cable needle and hold at front of work, P1 from left hand needle then K1 from cable needle, K1.
5th row K1, P2, (C2FP, P3) twice, P1, K1.
7th row K1, (P3, C2FP) twice, P3, K1.
9th row K2, (P3, C2FP) twice, P2, K1.
11th row K1, sl next st on to cable needle and hold at front of work, K1 from left hand needle then K1 from cable needle — abbreviated as CF—, (P3, C2FP) twice, P1, K1.
12th row As 2nd row.
These 12 rows form right panel.

Back
With No 8/4mm needles cast on 84[88:92:96] sts.
1st row (Rs) K3, *P2, K2, rep from * to last st, K1.
2nd row K1, *P2, K2, rep from * to last 3 sts, P2, K1.
Rep these 2 rows until back measures 3½in/9cm from beg, ending with a 2nd row.
Next row (inc row) Rib 0[2:4:6], (inc in next st, rib 1) 41 times, inc in next st, rib to end.
126[130:134:138] sts.
P one row.
Change to No 6/5mm needles.
Commence patt.
1st row (Rs) K1, (P1, K1) 5[6:6:7] times, P2, (CF, CB) twice see 11th row of left and right panels for abbreviation, P2, work 1st row of left panel, P2, sl next 2 sts on to cable needle and hold at back of work, K1 from left hand needle then K2 from cable needle; now sl next st on to cable needle and hold at front of work, K2 from left hand needle then K1 from cable needle — abbreviated as C6 —, P2, K into back of next st — abbreviated as K1B —, P1, K1B, P20[20:24:24] sts, K1B, P1, K1B, P2, C6, P2, work 1st row of right panel, P2, (CF, CB) twice, P2, (K1, P1) 5[6:6:7] times, K1.
2nd row P11[13:13:15], K2, P8, K2, work 2nd row of right panel, K2, P6, K2, P into back of next st — abbreviated as P1B —, K1, P1B, (P3 tog, K1, P1, K1 all into next st to make 3) 5[5:6:6] times, P1B, K1, P1B, K2, P6, K2, work 2nd row of left panel, K2, P8, K2, P to end.
3rd row K1, (P1, K1)5[6:6:7] times, P2, (CB, CF) twice, P2, work 3rd row of left panel, P2, K6, P2, K1B, P1, K1B, P20[20:24:24], K1B, P1, K1B, P2, K6, P2, work 3rd row of right panel, P2, (CB, CF) twice, P2, (K1, P1) 5[6:6:7] times, K1.
4th row P11[13:13:15], K2, P8, K2, work 4th row of right panel, K2, P6, K2, P1B, K1, P1B, (K1, P1, K1 all into next st, P3 tog) 5[5:6:6] times, P1B, K1, P1B, K2, P6, K2,

Pattern pieces

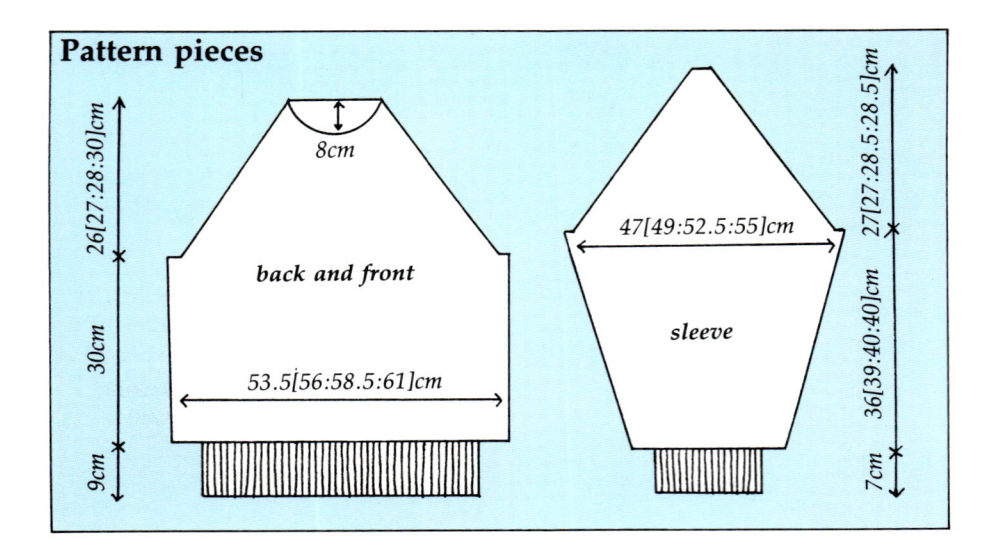

back and front: 26[27:28:30]cm, 30cm, 9cm, 8cm, 53.5[56:58.5:61]cm

sleeve: 27[27:28.5:28.5]cm, 47[49:52.5:55]cm, 36[39:40:40]cm, 7cm

work 4th row of left panel, K2, P8, K2, P to end.
5th to 12th rows Rep 1st to 4th rows twice, but working 5th to 12th rows of left and right panels as now set.
These 12 rows form patt.
Cont in patt until back measures 15½in/39cm from beg, ending with a Ws row.

Shape raglans
Keep patt correct throughout.
1st row Cast off 2 sts, patt to end.
2nd row Cast off 2 sts, patt to end.
3rd row K1, K2 tog tbl, patt to last 3 sts, K2 tog, K1.
4th row K1, P1, patt to last 2 sts, P1, K1.
Rep 3rd and 4th rows until 98[102:98:102] sts rem, ending after a 4th row.
Next row As 3rd row.
Next row K1, P2 tog, patt to last 3 sts, P2 tog tbl, K1.
Rep last 2 rows until 30[30:34:34] sts rem.
Leave sts on holder for centre back neck.

Front
Work as given for back until 54[58:62:66] sts rem in raglan shaping, ending with a Ws row.

Shape neck
Next row K1, K2 tog tbl, patt 15[17:17:19] sts, turn and leave rem sts on a spare needle.
Complete left side first.
Cont dec at raglan edge on every row, *at the same time* dec one st at neck edge on next 4 rows. 9[11:11:13] sts.

Cont dec at raglan edge only until 2 sts rem.
Next row Work 2 tog. Fasten off.
With Rs of work facing, sl first 18[18:22:22] sts from spare needle on to a holder and leave for centre front neck, rejoin yarn to rem sts and with Rs facing, patt to last 3 sts, K2 tog, K1.
Complete right side to match left side.

Sleeves
With No 8/4mm needles cast on 36[40:40:44] sts. Work 3in/7cm rib as given for back welt, ending with a 2nd row.
Next row (inc row) Rib 1[5:3:7] sts, inc one st in each of next 33[29:33:29] sts, rib to end. 69[69:73:73] sts.
P one row.
Change to No 6/5mm needles.
Commence patt.
1st row (Rs) K1, (P1, K1) 1[1:2:2] times, P2, work 1st row of left panel, P2, C6, P2, (K1B, P1) 3 times, P1, C6, P2, work 1st row of right panel, P2, (K1, P1) 1[1:2:2] times, K1.
2nd row P3[3:5:5], K2, work 2nd row of right panel, K2, P6, K2, (P1B, K1) 3 times, K1, P6, K2, work 2nd row of left panel, K2, P to end.
3rd row K1, (P1, K1) 1[1:2:2] times, P2, work 3rd row of left panel, P2, K6, P2, (K1B, P1) 3 times, P1, K6, P2, work 3rd row of right panel, P2, (K1, P1) 1[1:2:2] times, K1.
4th row As 2nd row but working 4th row of left and right panels.
5th to 12th rows Rep 1st to 4th rows twice, but working 5th to 12th rows of left and right panels.
These 12 rows form patt.
Cont in patt, inc one st at each end of next and every foll 8th[6th:6th:4th] row until there are 81[87:87:79] sts, then on every foll 10th[8th:8th:6th] row until there are 85[89:95:99] sts, taking extra sts into broken rib patt.
Cont without shaping until sleeve measures 17[18:18½:18½]in/ 43[46:47:47]cm from beg, ending with a Ws row.

Shape raglan
1st to 4th rows Work as given for back raglan shaping.
Rep 3rd and 4th rows only until 37[41:45:49] sts rem, ending after a 4th row.
Next row As 3rd row.
Next row K1, P2 tog, patt to last 3 sts, P2 tog tbl, K1.
Rep last 2 rows until 9 sts rem. Sl sts on to a spare needle.

Neckband (optional)
Join back, front and sleeves raglan shapings.
**With Rs of work facing and set of four No 8/4mm needles, K across sts of back neck dec 3[3:5:5] sts evenly, K across sts of left sleeve top, pick up and K10[12:14:14] sts down left side of front neck, K across front neck sts on holder dec 3[3:5:5] sts evenly, pick up and K10[12:14:14] sts up right side of front neck and K across sts of right sleeve top. 80[84:92:92] sts. **
Work in rounds of K2, P2 rib for 1¼[1¼:1½:1½]in/3[3:4:4] cm.
Cast off loosely in rib.

Polo collar (optional)
Work as given for neckband from ** to **.
Work in rounds of K2, P2 rib for 6½[6½:7:7]in/17[17:18:18]cm.
Cast off loosely in rib.

To make up
Press as given on ball band, omitting ribbing.
Join side and sleeve seams. Press seams.

Aran jersey

All the traditions of Aran knitting are incorporated into this design, which is suitable for a man or a woman.
The stitch patterns and Aran wool are authentic and the jersey features a dropped shoulder-line and neat, round neck.

Measurements

To fit 35 – 37[39 – 42]in/89 – 94[99 – 107]cm bust/chest
Actual measurements, 41[46]in/ 104[117]cm
Length to shoulders, 24[26]in/ 61[67]cm
Sleeve seam, 18[19]in/46[48]cm
The figures in [] refer to the 39 – 42in/99 – 107cm size only

Materials

8[9] × 100g balls of Robin Aran 100
One pair No 8/4mm needles
One pair No 6/5mm needles
Cable needle
The quantities of yarn given are based on average requirements and are approximate

Tension

19 sts and 26 rows to 4in/10cm over panel patt A worked on No 6/5mm needles

Panel pattern A

Worked over 13[19] sts.
1st foundation row (Rs) P1, (K5, P1) 2[3] times.
2nd foundation row K1, (P5, K1) 2[3] times.
Now work in main patt.
1st row P1, (K5, P1) 2[3] times.
2nd row K13[19] sts.
3rd row P1, (K5, P1) 2[3] times.
4th row K1, (P5, K1) 2[3] times.
These 4 rows form panel patt A.
Note: When knitting sleeves, panel patt A is worked over 7 sts only and the figs in brackets are worked once.

Panel pattern B

Worked over 10 sts.
1st foundation row (Rs) P3, K1, P6.
2nd foundation row K6, P1, K3.
Now work in main patt.
1st row P1, (P1, K1, P1) all into next st making 3 sts from 1, turn, K3, turn, P3 then sl 2nd and 3rd sts over first st and off needle to complete bobble — abbreviated as MB —, P1, sl next st on to cable needle and hold at front of work, P1 from left hand needle then K1 from cable needle — abbreviated as C2L —, P5.
2nd row K5, P1, K4.
3rd row P4, C2L, P4.
4th row K4, P1, K5.
5th row P5, C2L, P3.
6th row K3, P1, K6.
7th row P6, C2L, P2.
8th row K2, P1, K7.
9th row P6, sl next st on to cable needle and hold at back of work, K1 from left hand needle then P1 from cable needle — abbreviated as C2R —, P1, MB.
10th row K3, P1, K6.
11th row P5, C2R, P3.
12th row K4, P1, K5.
13th row P4, C2R, P4.
14th row K5, P1, K4.
15th row P3, C2R, P5.
16th row K6, P1, K3.
These 16 rows form panel patt B.

Panel pattern C

Worked over 20 sts.
1st foundation row (Rs) (P2, K7) twice, P2.
2nd foundation row (K2, P7) twice, K2.
Now work in main patt.
1st row (P2, sl next 2 sts on to cable needle and hold at back of work, K1 from left hand needle then K2 from cable needle, K1, sl next st on to cable needle and hold at front of work, K2 from left hand needle then K1 from cable needle) twice, P2.
2nd row (K2, P7) twice, K2.
3rd row (P2, K7) twice, P2.

Pattern pieces

back and front: 52[58.5]cm wide, 53[59]cm tall, 8cm ribbing, neck 22[24]cm wide, 7cm deep
sleeves: 48[50.5]cm wide at top, 38[40]cm tall, 8cm ribbing

4th row (K2, P7) twice, K2.
These 4 rows form panel patt C.

Panel pattern D
Worked over 34 sts.
1st foundation row (Rs) (P4, K2) 5 times, P4.
2nd foundation row (K4, sl next st on to cable needle and hold at front of work, P1 from left hand needle then P1 from cable needle — abbreviated as Tw2P) 5 times, K4.
Now work in main patt.
1st row P3, (C2R, C2L, P2) 5 times, P1.
2nd row K3, (P1, K2) 10 times, K1.
3rd row P2, (C2R, P2, C2L) 5 times, P2.
4th row K2, P1, K4, (Tw2P, K4) 4 times, P1, K2.
5th row P2, (C2L, P2, C2R) 5 times, P2.
6th row K3, (P1, K2) 10 times, K1.
7th row P3, (C2L, C2R, P2) 5 times, P1.
8th row K4, (Tw2P, K4) 5 times.
These 8 rows form panel patt D.

Back
With No 8/4mm needles cast on 116[128] sts. Commence twisted rib for welt.
1st row (Rs) *K next st tbl, P1, rep from * to end.
Rep this row 18 times more.
Next row (inc row) Rib 24[30] sts, M1 by picking up loop lying between needles and K tbl, rib 15, M1, rib 38, M1, rib 15, M1, rib 24[30] sts. 120[132] sts.
Change to No 6/5mm needles.
Commence patt placing patt panels as foll:
1st foundation row (Rs) Work 1st foundation row of panel patt A, work 1st foundation row of panel patt B, work 1st foundation row of panel patt C, work 1st foundation row of panel patt D, work 1st foundation row of panel patt C, work 1st foundation row of panel patt B and, finally, work 1st foundation row of panel patt A.
2nd foundation row Work 2nd foundation row panel patt A, work 2nd foundation row panel patt B, work 2nd foundation row panel patt C, work 2nd foundation row panel patt D, work 2nd foundation row panel patt C, work 2nd foundation row panel patt B and, finally, work 2nd foundation row panel patt A.
Now work in main patt as foll:
1st row Work 1st row panel patt A, work 1st row panel patt B, work 1st row panel patt C, work 1st row panel patt D, work 1st row panel patt C, work 1st row panel patt B, work 1st row panel patt A.
Cont in patt as now set, working appropriate rows of each panel patt, until back measures 24[26½]in/61[67]cm from beg, ending with a Ws row.

Shape shoulders
Cast off 13[14] sts at beg of next 4 rows and 13[15] sts at beg of foll 2 rows.
Leave rem 42[46] sts on a holder for centre back neck.

Front
Work as given for back until front measures 21½[24]in/55[61]cm from beg, ending with a Ws row.

Shape neck
Keep patt correct throughout.
Next row Patt 49[53] sts, turn and leave rem sts on a spare needle. Complete left shoulder first.
Dec one st at neck edge on every row until 39[43] sts rem.
Cont without shaping until front measures same as back to shoulder, ending at side edge.

Shape shoulder
Cast off 13[14] sts at beg of next and foll alt row. Work one row.
Cast off rem 13[15] sts.
With Rs of work facing, sl first 22[26] sts from spare needle on to holder and leave for centre front neck, rejoin yarn to rem sts and patt to end. 49[53] sts.
Complete right shoulder to match left shoulder, noting that an extra row will have to be worked before beg of shoulder shaping.

Sleeves
With No 8/4mm needles cast on 44 sts for both sizes. Work 17 rows twisted rib as given for back welt.
Next row (inc row) Rib 2, M1 as given for back, rib 2, M1, rib 36, M1, rib 2, M1, rib 2. 48 sts.
Change to No 6/5mm needles.
Commence patt placing patt panels as foll:
1st foundation row (Rs) Work 7[7] sts as 1st foundation row panel patt A, work 1st foundation row panel patt D, work 7[7] sts as 1st foundation row panel patt A.
2nd foundation row Work 7[7] sts as 2nd foundation row panel patt A, work 2nd foundation row panel patt D, work 7[7] sts as 2nd foundation row panel patt A.
Now work in main patt as foll:
1st row Work 7[7] sts as 1st row panel patt A, work 1st row panel patt D, work 7[7] sts as 1st row panel patt A.
Cont in patt as now set, working appropriate row of panels A and D for 3 rows. Cont in patt, inc one st at each end of next and every foll 4th row until there are 92[96] sts, working extra sts into panel patt A.
Cont without shaping until sleeve measures 18[19]in/46[48]cm from beg, ending with a Ws row.
Cast off loosely in patt.

Neckband
Join right shoulder seam.
With Rs of work facing and No 8/4mm needles, pick up and K20[20] sts down left side of front neck, K22[26] sts from front neck holder, pick up and K20[20] sts up right front neck then K42[46] sts from back neck holder. 104[112] sts.
Work 7 rows twisted rib as given for back welt.
Cast off in rib.

To make up
Do not press.
Join left shoulder and neckband seam.
Fold sleeves in half lengthways, with fold to shoulder seam, sew sleeves in place.
Join side and sleeve seams.

Opposite: The simple shape of this Aran jersey means that you can avoid complicated shaping when working the panels of authentic patterns. It has a neat, round neckline and dropped shoulders. Designed by Maureen Briggs.

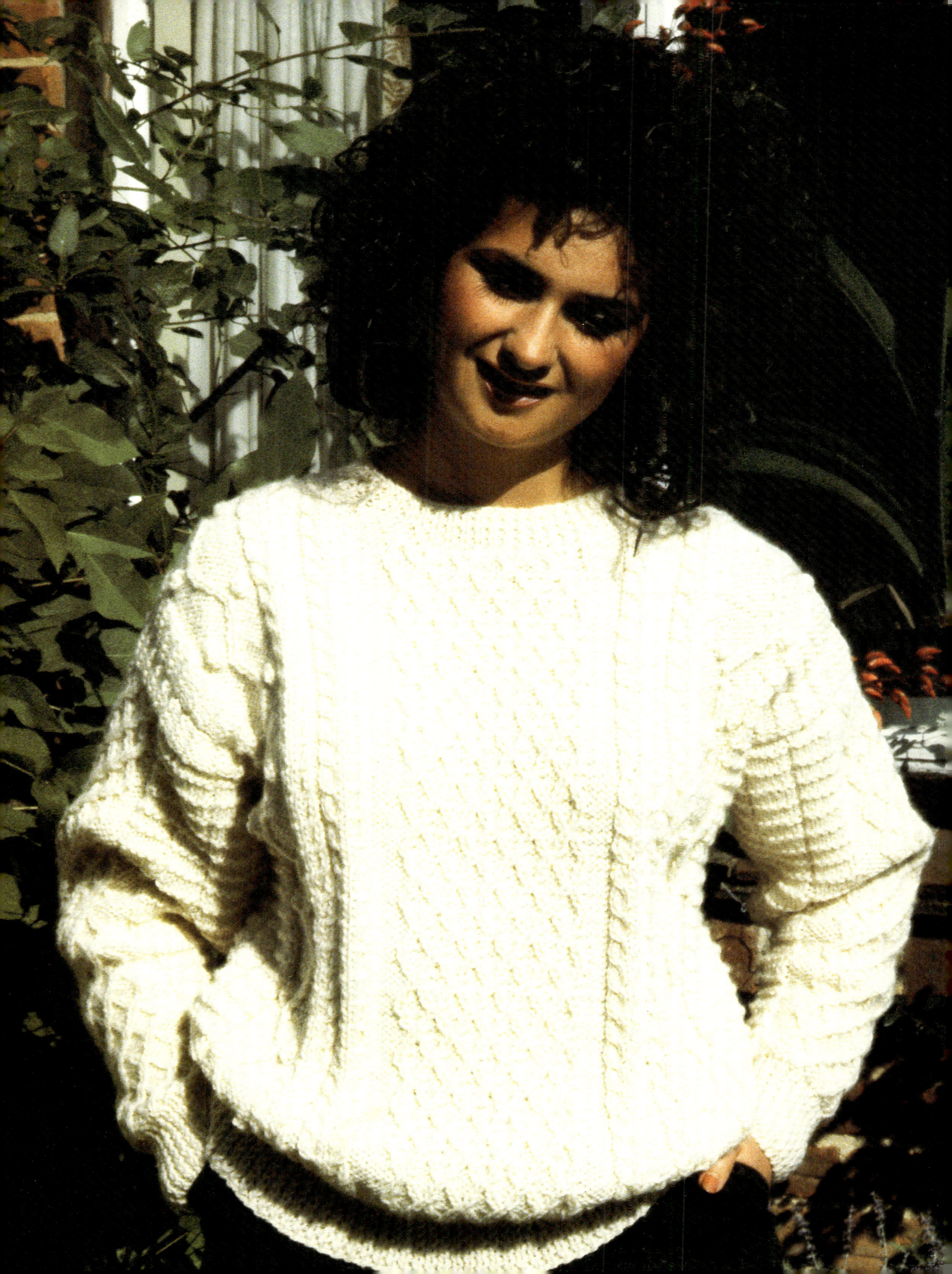

Random dyed Aran jersey

This design has a dropped shoulder line and is suitable for a man or woman.
It is not as highly textured as some Aran garments but relies for effect on an unusual random-dyed yarn, which lifts it into the couture class.

Measurements
To fit 36[38:40:42:44]in/ 91[97:102:107:112]cm bust/chest loosely
Actual measurements, 42[43½:46:47½:50½]in/ 107[110:117:121:128]cm
Length to shoulders, 25½[26½:27:27¼:27½]in/ 65[67:68:69:70]cm
Sleeve seam, 19[19½:19½:19½:19½]in/ 48[49:49:49:49]cm
The figures in [] refer to the 38/97, 40/102, 42/107 and 44in/112cm sizes respectively

Materials
11[11:12:12:13] × 50g balls of Jaeger Prelude Peacocks Double Knitting
One pair No 10/3¼mm needles
One pair No 8/4mm needles
Cable needle
The quantities of yarn given are based on average requirements and are approximate

Tension
22 sts and 30 rows to 4in/10cm over st st worked on No 8/4mm needles

Panel pattern A
Worked over 22 sts.
1st row (Rs) P9, K4, P9.
2nd and every alt row K all K sts and P all P sts, noting that this row will read K9, P4, K9.
3rd row P7, sl next 2 sts on to a cable needle and hold at back of work, K2 from left hand needle then P2 from cable needle — abbreviated as Cr4BP —, sl next 2 sts on to a cable needle and hold at front of work, P2 from left hand needle then K2 from cable needle — abbreviated as Cr4FP —, P7.
5th row P7, K2, P4, K2, P7.
7th row P5, Cr4BP, P4, Cr4FP, P5.
9th row P5, K2, P8, K2, P5.
11th row P3, Cr4BP, P8, Cr4FP, P3.
13th row P3, K2, P12, K2, P3.
15th row As 13th row.
17th row P3, Cr4FP, P8, Cr4BP, P3.
19th row As 9th row.
21st row P5, Cr4FP, P4, Cr4BP, P5.
23rd row As 5th row.
25th row P7, Cr4FP, Cr4BP, P7.
26th row As 2nd row.
These 26 rows form panel patt A.

Panel pattern B
Worked over 14 sts.
1st row (Rs) P3, K8, P3.
2nd and every alt row K all K sts and P all P sts, noting that this row will read K3, P8, K3.
3rd row P3, sl next 2 sts on to cable needle and hold at back of work, K2 from left hand needle then K2 from cable needle — abbreviated as C4B —, sl next 2 sts on to cable needle and hold at front of work, K2 from left hand needle then K2 from cable needle — called C4F —, P3.
5th, 7th and 9th rows As 1st row.
11th row P3, C4F, C4B, P3.
12th row As 2nd row.
These 12 rows form panel patt B.

Panel pattern C
Worked over 38 sts.
1st row (Rs) K tog next 2 sts on left hand needle but do not sl sts off needle, K the first of these 2 sts again and sl both sts off needle — abbreviated as Sp2F —, P12, K10, P12, Sp2F.
2nd row P2, K12, P10, K12, P2.
3rd row Sp2F, P12, K2, P1, K into back of next st — abbreviated as KB1 —, P2, KB1, P1, K2, P12, Sp2F.
4th row P2, K12, P2, K1, P into back of next st — abbreviated as PB1 —, K2, PB1, K1, P2, K12, P2.
5th row Sp2F, P10, Cr4BP (see 3rd row patt A), P1, KB1, P2, KB1, P1, Cr4FP (see 3rd row patt A), P10, Sp2F.
6th row P2, K10, P2, K3, PB1, K2, PB1, K3, P2, K10, P2.
7th row Sp2F, P10, K2, P3, KB1, P2, KB1, P3, K2, P10, Sp2F.
8th row As 6th row.
9th row Sp2F, P8, Cr4BP, (KB1, P2) 3 times, KB1, Cr4FP, P8, Sp2F.
10th row P2, K8, P2, (K2, PB1) 4 times, K2, 2, K8, P2.
11th row Sp2F, P8, K2, (P2, KB1) 4 times, P2, K2, P8, Sp2F.
12th row As 10th row.
13th row Sp2F, P6, Cr4BP, (P2, KB1) 4 times, P2, Cr4FP, P6, Sp2F.
14th row P2, K6, P2, K4, (PB1, K2) 4 times, K2, P2, K6, P2.
15th row Sp2F, P6, K2, P1, (KB1, P2) 5 times, KB1, P1, K2, P6, Sp2F.
16th row P2, K6, P2, K1, (PB1, P2) 5 times, PB1, K1, P2, K6, P2.
17th row Sp2F, P4, Cr4BP, P1, (KB1, P2) 5 times, KB1, P1, Cr4FP, P4, Sp2F.
18th row P2, K4, P2, K3, (PB1, K2) 5 times, PB1, K3, P2, K4, P2.
19th row Sp2F, P4, K2, P3, (KB1, P2) 5 times, KB1, P3, K2, P4, Sp2F.
20th row As 18th row.
21st row As 19th row.
22nd row As 18th row.
23rd row Sp2F, P34, Sp2F.
24th row P2, K34, P2.
These 24 rows form panel patt C.

Back
With No 10/3¼mm needles cast on 101[107:113:117:123] sts.
1st row (Rs) K1, *P1, K1, rep from * to end.
2nd row P1, *K1, P1, rep from * to end.
Rep these 2 rows until back measures 2¾in/7cm from beg, ending with a 1st row.

Opposite: Twisted stitches and cables have been used for this jersey, which has a round neckband and dropped shoulder-line. Whilst the patterns are traditional, an unusual effect is achieved by the use of a modern, random-dyed yarn. Designed by Debbie Jenkins.

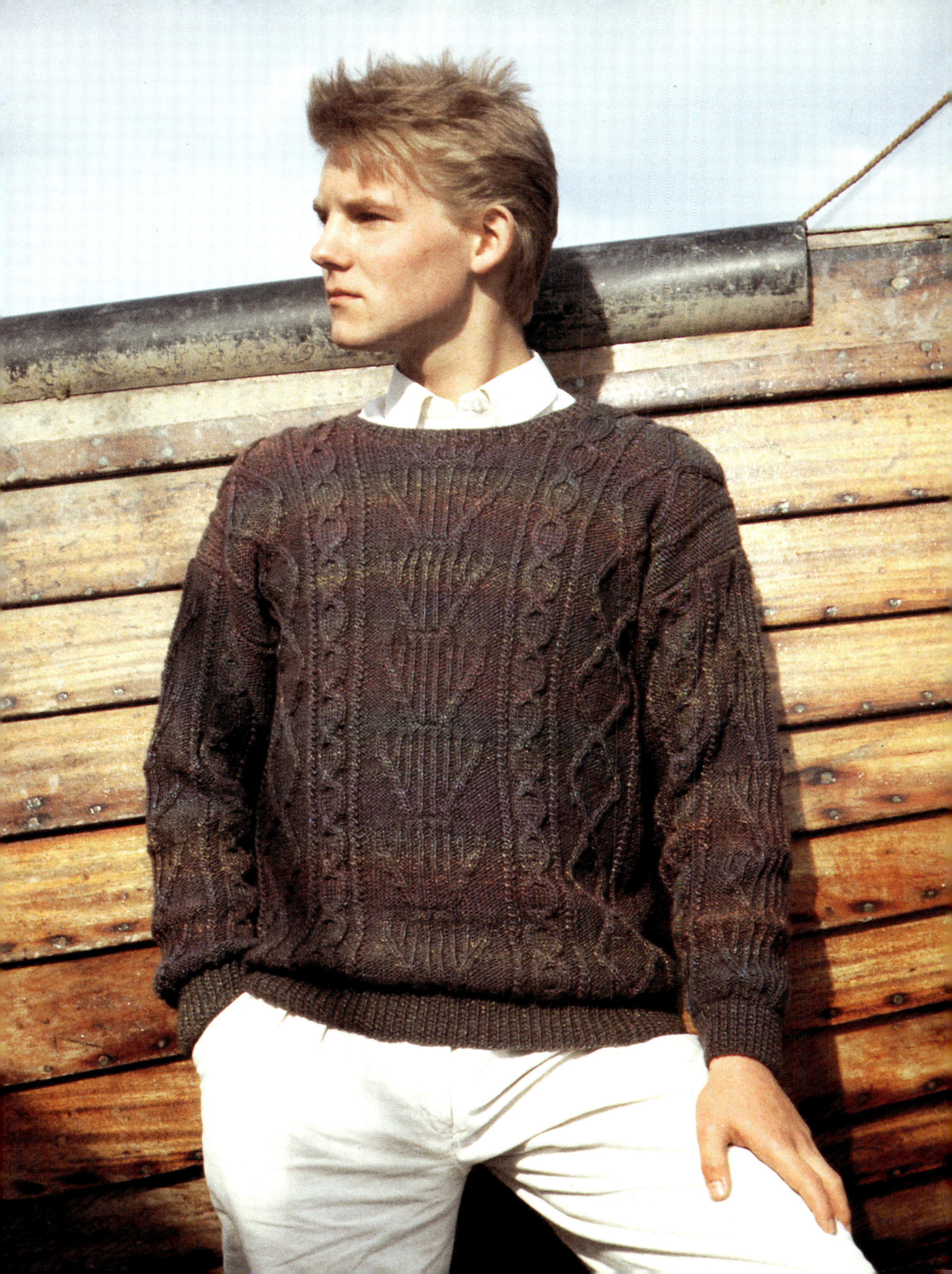

Next row (inc row) Rib 7[4:2:4:2] sts, *M1 by picking up loop lying between needles and K tbl, rib 4[5:5:5:5], rep from * to last 6[3:1:3:1] sts, M1, rib to end. 124[128:136:140:148] sts.
Change to No 8/4mm needles.
Commence patt, placing patt panels as foll:
1st row (Rs) P3[5:9:11:15] sts, Sp2F (see 1st row patt C), work 1st row panel patt A, Sp2F, work 1st row panel patt B, work 1st row panel patt C, work 1st row panel patt B, Sp2F, work 1st row as panel patt A, Sp2F, P to end.
2nd row K3[5:9:11:15] sts, P2, work 2nd row as panel patt A, P2, work 2nd row as panel patt B, work 2nd row as panel patt C, work 2nd row as panel patt B, P2, work 2nd row as panel patt A, P2, K to end.
Cont in patt as now set, working appropriate rows of each panel patt, until back measures 25½[26½:27:27¼:27½]in/ 65[67:68:69:70]cm from beg, ending with a Ws row.

Shape shoulders
Cast off 10[11:12:12:13] sts at beg of next 6 rows, then 11[10:10:12:13] sts at beg of foll 2 rows.
Leave rem 42[42:44:44:44] sts on a spare needle for centre back neck.

Front
Work as given for back until front measures 22[22:24:24:24] rows less than back to shoulder, ending with a Ws row.

Shape neck
Keep patt correct throughout.
Next row Patt 52[54:58:60:64] sts, turn and leave rem sts on a spare needle.
Complete left shoulder first.
Dec one st at beg of next row and at same edge 5[5:7:7:7] times.
Work one row.
Dec one st at neck edge on next and every foll alt row until 41[43:46:48:52] sts rem.
Work 4[4:6:6:6] rows without shaping, ending with a Ws row.

Shape shoulder
Cast off 10[11:12:12:13] sts at beg of next and foll 2 alt rows. Work one row.
Cast off rem 11[10:10:12:13] sts.

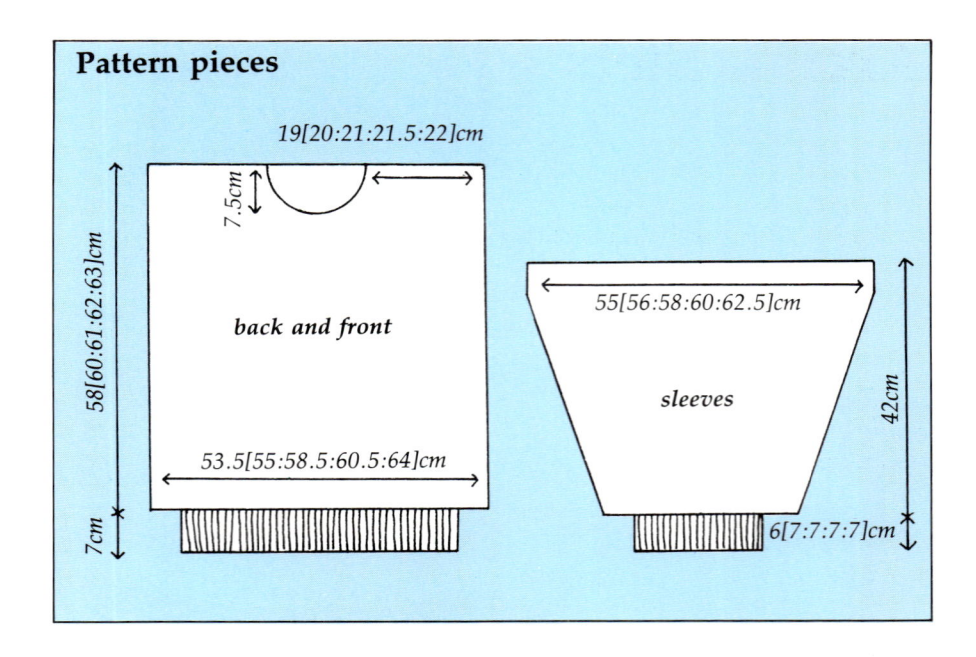

Pattern pieces

back and front: 58[60:61:62:63]cm high, 53.5[55:58.5:60.5:64]cm wide, neck 19[20:21:21.5:22]cm wide × 7.5cm deep, rib 7cm.

sleeves: 55[56:58:60:62.5]cm top, 42cm long, cuff 6[7:7:7:7]cm rib.

With Rs of work facing, sl first 20 sts from spare needle on to a holder and leave for centre front neck, rejoin yarn to rem sts and patt to end.
Complete right shoulder to match left, reversing all shapings and noting that an extra row will have to be worked before beg of shoulder shaping.

Sleeves
With No 10/3¼mm needles cast on 55[55:55:57:57] sts. Work 2¼[2¾:2¾:2¾:2¾]in/6[7:7:7:7]cm rib as given for back, ending with a 1st row.
Next row (inc row) Rib 2[2:2:5:5] sts, *M1 as given for back, rib 2, rep from * to last 1[1:1:4:4] sts, M1, rib to end. 82 sts.
Change to No 8/4mm needles.
Commence patt placing patt panels as foll:
1st row (Rs) P4, Sp2F, P1, work 1st row panel patt B, P1, work 1st row panel patt C, P1, work 1st row panel patt B, P1, Sp2F, P to end.
2nd row K4, P2, K1, work 2nd row as panel patt B, K1, work 2nd row as panel patt C, K1, work 2nd row as panel patt B, K1, P2, K to end.
Cont in patt as now set, working appropriate rows of each panel patt, *at the same time* inc one st at each end of 11th[5th:5th:5th:5th] row from beg of patt and every foll 6th row until there are 120[120:112:104:92] sts, taking extra sts into rev st st.

2nd, 3rd, 4th and 5th sizes only
Work 3 rows without shaping.
Inc one st at each end of next and every foll 4th row until there are [124:128:132:138] sts, taking extra sts into rev st st.

All sizes
Work 7[5:5:5:5] rows, ending with a Ws row.
Cast off loosely.

Neckband
Join right shoulder seam.
With Rs of work facing and No 10/3¼mm needles, pick up and K18[18:22:22:22] sts down left side of front neck, K20 sts from front neck holder, pick up and K18[18:22:22:22] sts up right front neck, then K42[42:44:44:44] sts from back neck holder, inc one st in centre. 99[99:109:109:109] sts.
Beg and ending with a 2nd row, work ¾in/2cm rib as given for back.
Cast off in rib.

To make up
Do not press.
Join left shoulder and neckband seam.
Fold sleeves in half lengthways, with fold to shoulder seam, sew in place.
Join side and sleeve seams.

Aran jackets

This comfortable jacket can be worked as a low-buttoning version for a woman, or a shawl-collared version for a man. It features a dropped shoulder-line and inset pockets on the fronts.
The yarn used for this design comes in a range of soft, muted colours, or you can use the traditional off-white shade.

Measurements
To fit 34–36[38–40:42–44]in/86–91[97–102:107–112]cm bust/chest
Actual measurements, 42[46:50]in/107[117:127]cm
Length to shoulders, 24½[26:27½]in/62[66:70]cm
Sleeve seam, 18[19:19]in/46[48:48]cm
The figures in [] refer to the 38–40/97–102 and 42–44/107–112cm sizes respectively

Materials
Low-buttoning version, 8[10:11] × 100g balls of Robin Aran 100
Shawl collared version, 9[10:11] balls of same
One pair No 8/4mm needles
One pair No 6/5mm needles
Cable needle
Four buttons
The quantities of yarn given are based on average requirements and are approximate

Tension
19 sts and 26 rows to 4in/10cm over panel patt A worked on No 6/5mm needles

Panel pattern A
Worked over multiples of 2 sts plus 1.
1st row (Rs) *P1, K1, rep from * to last st, P1.
2nd row *K1, P1, rep from * to last st, K1.
3rd row *K1, P1, rep from * to last st, K1.
4th row *P1, K1, rep from * to last st, P1.
These 4 rows form panel patt A.

Note: The number of sts in panel A will vary for the different panels

Panel pattern B
Worked over 37 sts.
1st row (Rs) P2, K4, P10, sl next st on to cable needle and hold at back of work, K1 tbl from left hand needle then P1 from cable needle — abbreviated as Tw2R —, K1, sl next st on to cable needle and hold at front of work, P1 from left hand needle then K1 tbl from cable needle — abbreviated as Tw2L —, P10, K4, P2.
2nd row K2, P4, K10, (P1, K1) twice, P1, K10, P4, K2.
3rd row P2, sl next 2 sts on to cable needle and hold at back of work, K2 from left hand needle then K2 from cable needle — abbreviated as C4B —, P9, Tw2R, K1, P1, K1, Tw2L, P9, sl next 2 sts on to cable needle and hold at front of work, K2 from left hand needle then K2 from cable needle — abbreviated as C4F —, P2.
4th row K2, P4, K9, (P1, K1) 3 times, P1, K9, P4, K2.
5th row P2, K4, P8, Tw2R, (K1, P1) twice, K1, Tw2L, P8, K4, P2.
6th row K2, P4, K8, (P1, K1) 4 times, P1, K8, P4, K2.
7th row P2, C4B, P7, Tw2R, (K1, P1) 3 times, K1, Tw2L, P7, C4F, P2.
8th row K2, P4, K7, (P1, K1) 5 times, P1, K7, P4, K2.
9th row P2, K4, P6, Tw2R, (K1, P1) 4 times, K1, Tw2L, P6, K4, P2.
10th row K2, P4, K6, (P1, K1) 6 times, P1, K6, P4, K2.
11th row P2, C4B, P5, Tw2R, (K1, P1) 5 times, K1, Tw2L, P5, C4F, P2.
12th row K2, P4, K5, (P1, K1) 7 times, P1, K5, P4, K2.
13th row P2, K4, P4, Tw2R, (K1, P1) 6 times, K1, Tw2L, P4, K4, P2.
14th row K2, P4, K4, (P1, K1) 8 times, P1, K4, P4, K2.
15th row P2, C4B, P3, Tw2R, (K1, P1) 7 times, K1, Tw2L, P3, C4F, P2.
16th row K2, P4, K3, (P1, K1) 9 times, P1, K3, P4, K2.
17th row P2, K4, P3, Tw2L, (P1, K1) 7 times, P1, Tw2R, P3, K4, P2.
18th row K2, P4, K4, (P1, K1) 8 times, P1, K4, P4, K2.
19th row P2, C4B, P4, Tw2L, (P1, K1) 6 times, P1, Tw2R, P4, C4F, P2.
20th row K2, P4, K5, (P1, K1) 7 times, P1, K5, P4, K2.
21st row P2, K4, P5, Tw2L, (P1, K1) 5 times, P1, Tw2R, P5, K4, P2.
22nd row K2, P4, K6, (P1, K1) 6 times, P1, K6, P4, K2.
23rd row P2, C4B, P6, Tw2L, (P1, K1) 4 times, P1, Tw2R, P6, C4F, P2.
24th row K2, P4, K7, (P1, K1) 5 times, P1, K7, P4, K2.
25th row P2, K4, P7, Tw2L, (P1, K1) 3 times, P1, Tw2R, P7, K4, P2.
26th row K2, P4, K8, (P1, K1) 4 times, P1, K8, P4, K2.
27th row P2, C4B, P8, Tw2L, (P1, K1) twice, P1, Tw2R, P8, C4F, P2.
28th row K2, P4, K9, (P1, K1) 3 times, P1, K9, P4, K2.
29th row P2, K4, P9, Tw2L, P1, K1, P1, Tw2R, P9, K4, P2.
30th row K2, P4, K10, (P1, K1) twice, P1, K10, P4, K2.
31st row P2, C4B, P10, Tw2L, P1, Tw2R, P10, C4F, P2.
32nd row K2, P4, K11, sl next 2 sts on to cable needle and hold at front of work, P1 from left hand needle, sl 2nd st on cable needle back on to left hand needle and K it, then P rem st on cable needle, K11, P4, K2.
These 32 rows form panel patt B.

Back
With No 8/4mm needles cast on 115[125:133] sts. Commence twisted rib.
1st row (Rs) K1 tbl — abbreviated as K1B —, *P1, K1B, rep from * to end
2nd row P1, *K1B, P1, rep from * to end.
Rep these 2 rows 7[8:9] times more, then 1st row once more.
Next row (inc row) Rib 14[16:18] sts, *M1 by picking up loop lying between needles and K tbl, rib 29, M1, rib 29[35:39], M1, rib 29, M1, rib 14[16:18]. 119[129:137] sts.
Change to No 6/5mm needles.
Commence patt, placing patt panels as foll:

Pattern pieces

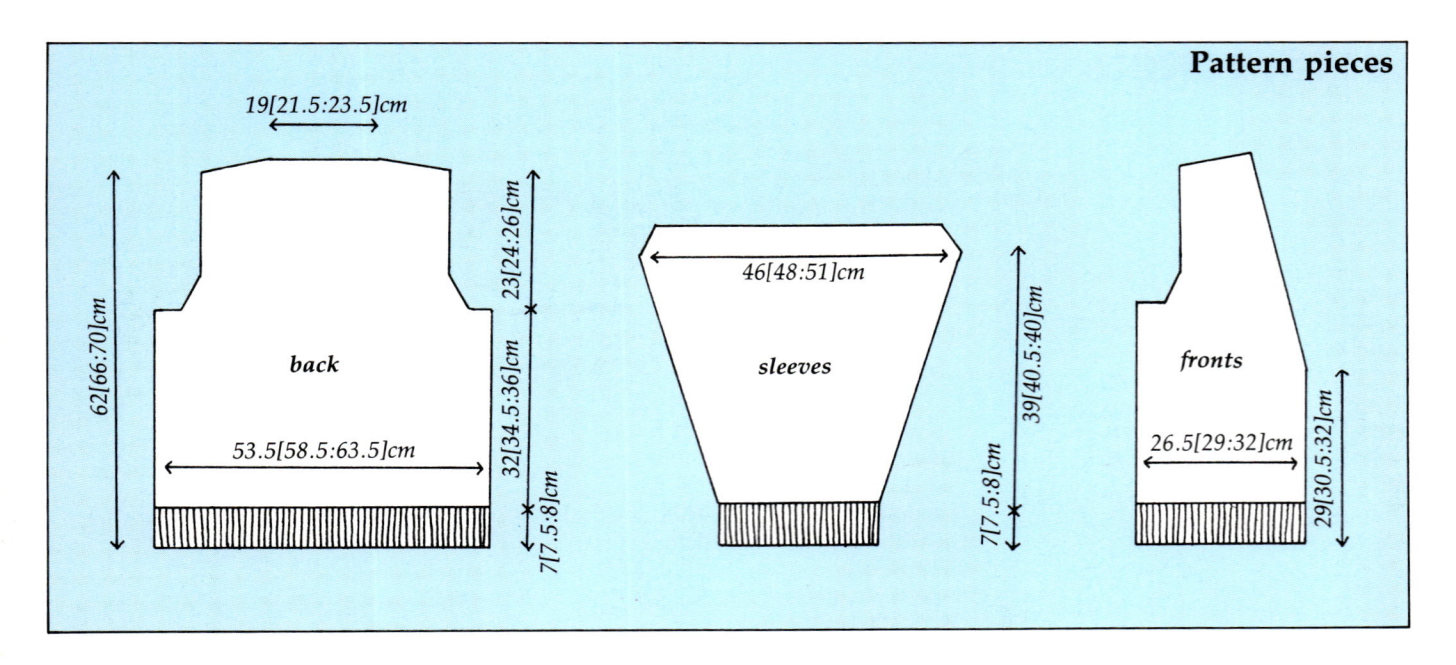

Diagram measurements:
- **back**: 19[21.5:23.5]cm (top), 53.5[58.5:63.5]cm (bottom), 62[66:70]cm (total height), 32[34.5:36]cm (side to armhole), 23[24:26]cm (armhole to shoulder), 7[7.5:8]cm (welt)
- **sleeves**: 46[48:51]cm (top), 39[40.5:40]cm (height), 7[7.5:8]cm (cuff)
- **fronts**: 26.5[29:32]cm (width), 29[30.5:32]cm (side height), 39[40.5:40]cm

1st row (Rs) Work 11[13:15] sts as 1st row panel patt A, work 1st row panel patt B, work 23[29:33] sts as 1st row panel patt A, work 1st row panel patt B, work 11[13:15] sts as 1st row panel patt A.
2nd row Work 11[13:15] sts as 2nd row of panel patt A, work 2nd row panel patt B, work 23[29:33] sts as 2nd row of panel patt A, work 2nd row panel patt B, work 11[13:15] sts as 2nd row panel patt A.
Cont in patt as now set, working appropriate rows of each panel patt, until back measures 15½[16½:17½]in/39[42:43]cm from beg, ending with a Ws row.

Shape armholes
Keeping patt correct throughout, cast off 5[6:7] sts at beg of next 2 rows, then dec one st at each end of next 4 Rs row. 101[109:115] sts.
Cont without shaping in patt until armholes measure 9[9½:10]in/23[24:25]cm from beg of shaping, ending with a Ws row.

Shape shoulders
Cast off 11[11:11] sts at beg of next 4 rows, then 11[12:13] sts at beg of foll 2 rows.
Cast off rem 35[41:45] sts.

Pocket back (work 2)
With No 6/5mm needles cast on 25 sts for all sizes.
Work 22 rows in panel patt A.
Leave sts on holder for time being.

Left front
With No 8/4mm needles cast on 57[61:65] sts. Work 17[19:21] rows in twisted rib as given for back welt.
Next row (inc row) Rib 14[16:18] sts, M1 as given for back, rib 29, M1, rib 14[16:18] sts. 59[63:67] sts.
Change to No 6/5mm needles. Commence patt, placing patt panels as foll:
1st row (Rs) Work 11[13:15] sts as 1st row of panel patt A, work 1st row panel patt B, work 11[13:15] sts as 1st row panel patt A.
2nd row Work 11[13:15] sts as 2nd row of panel patt A, work 2nd row of panel patt B, work 11[13:15] sts as 2nd row of panel patt A.
Cont in patt as now set, working appropriate rows of each panel patt until 24 patt rows have been worked.

Place pocket
Next row Work 11[13:15] sts of panel patt A, work first 6 sts of 25th row of panel patt B, sl next 25 sts on to a holder and leave for pocket top, in their place patt across 25 sts from pocket back, work last 6 sts of 25th row of panel patt B, work 11[13:15] sts of panel patt A.
Cont in patt without shaping until front measures 11½[12:12½]in/29[30:32]cm from beg, ending with a Ws row.

Shape front edge
Dec one st at front edge on next row and every foll 4th row until front measures same as back to underarm, ending at side edge.

Shape armhole
Cont dec at front edge on every 4th row as before, shape armhole by casting off 5[6:7] sts at beg of next row and dec one st at armhole edge on next 4 Rs rows. This completes armhole shaping.
Cont to dec at front edge only on every 4th row until 33[34:35] sts rem.
Cont in patt without shaping until front measures same as back to shoulder, ending at armhole edge.

Shape shoulder
Cast off 11[11:11] sts at beg of next and foll alt row. Work one row then cast off rem 11[12:13] sts.

*Opposite: Stylish jackets for a man or woman, worked in an authentic Aran yarn and featuring traditional patterns. Her version is shown with front bands which continue to form the back neckband and his has a snug shawl collar, but you can easily reverse these if you prefer.
Designed by Maureen Briggs.*

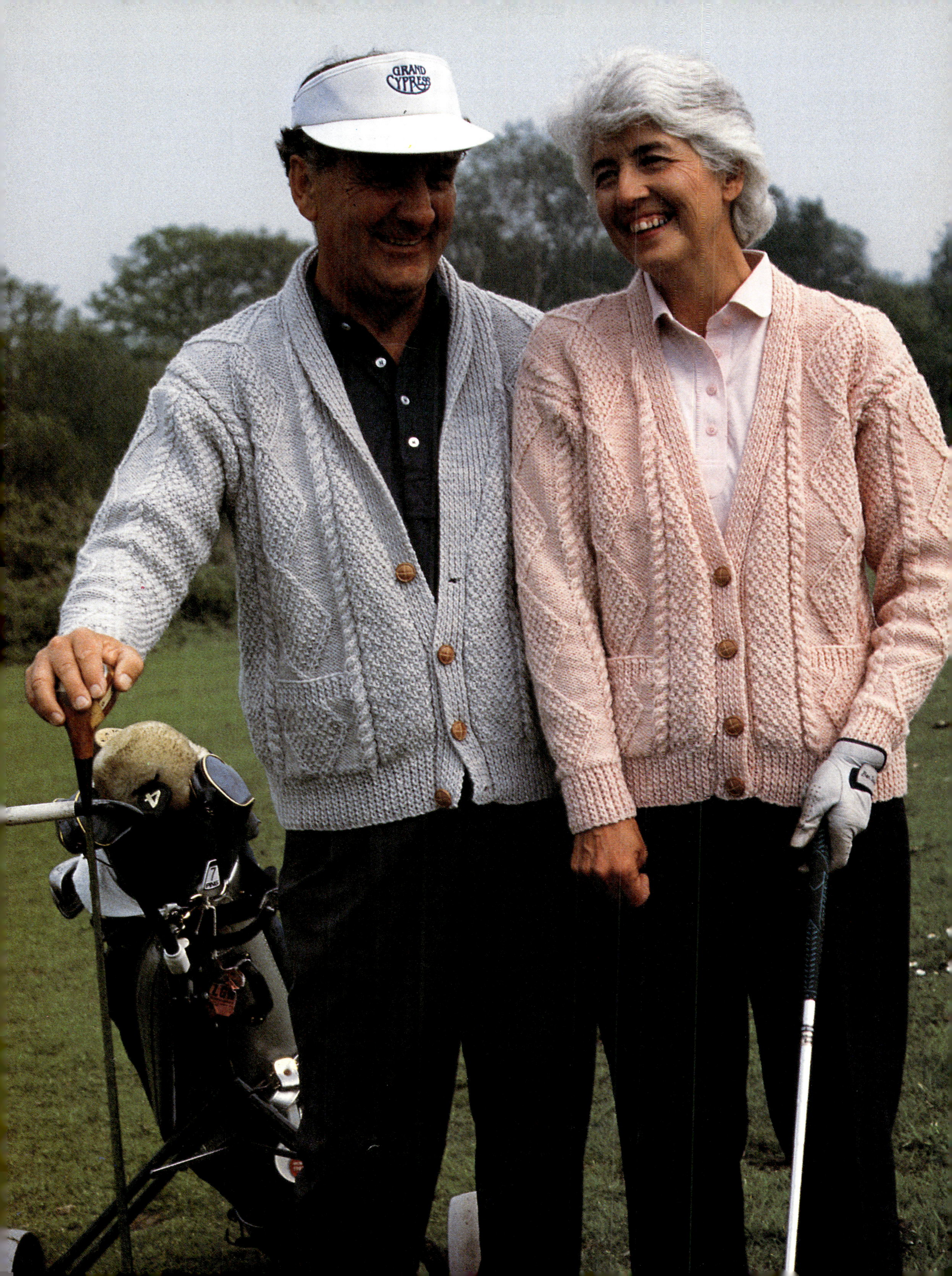
GRAND
CYPRESS

Right front
Work as given for left front, reversing all shaping.

Sleeves
With No 8/4mm needles cast on 41[45:49] sts. Work 17[19:21] rows twisted rib as given for back welt.
Next row (inc row) Rib 6[8:10] sts, M1 as given for back, rib 29, M1, rib 6[8:10] sts. 43[47:51] sts.
Change to No 6/5mm needles.
Commence patt, placing panel patts as foll:
1st row (Rs) Work 3[5:7] sts as 1st row of panel patt A, work 1st row panel patt B, work 3[5:7] sts as 1st row of panel patt A.
2nd row Work 3[5:7] sts as 2nd row of panel patt A, work 2nd row of panel patt B, work 3[5:7] sts as 2nd row of panel patt A.
Cont in patt as now set, working appropriate rows of each panel patt, *at the same time* inc one st at each end of next row and every foll 4th row until there are 87[91:95] sts, working extra sts into panel patt A.
Cont in patt without shaping until sleeve measures 18[19:19]in/ 46[48:48]cm from beg, ending with a Ws row.

Shape top
Place markers at each end of last row, then work 6[6:8] rows in patt without shaping.
Dec one st at each end of next 4 Rs rows. Work one row without shaping.
Cast off loosely.

Shawl collar (optional)
Join shoulder seams.
With No 8/4mm needles cast on 11 sts for button band and collar. Work in twisted rib as given for back welt until band, when slightly stretched, fits up front edge to beg of front shaping, ending at inside edge. Pin in place.

Shape collar
Cont in twisted rib, inc one st at beg of next and every foll 4th row until there are 31[33:35] sts, working extra sts into twisted rib.
Cont without shaping until collar, when slightly stretched, fits up shaped front edge and round to centre back neck. Cast off.
Sew band and collar in position.
Mark 4 button position on button band, first to come 2 rows above cast on edge and 4th to come 2 rows below beg of front shaping, with 2 more equally spaced between.
Work buttonhole band and collar as given for button band, making buttonholes as markers are reached as foll:
1st buttonhole row (Rs) Rib 4, cast off 3 sts, rib to end.
2nd buttonhole row Rib 4, cast on 3 sts, rib to end.

Ribbed front bands (optional)
Work as given for button and buttonhole bands on shawl collar version from ** to **, then cont without shaping until band fits up front shaping and round to centre back neck. Cast off.
Sew bands in position.

Pocket tops (make 2)
With Rs of work facing and No 8/4mm needles, P1, (K1B, P1) 12 times across 25 sts of pocket tops on holders.
Work 5 rows in twisted rib. Cast off in rib.

To make up
Do not press.
Set in sleeves, sewing row ends above markers on sleeves to the sts cast off for armholes on back and fronts.
Join side and sleeve seams.
Sew down pocket backs to Ws, then catch down row ends of pocket tops.
Join cast off edges of collar or bands at centre back neck.
Sew on buttons.

Abbreviations, conversions and needle sizes

Knitting abbreviations

alt	alternate(ly)
approx	approximate(ly)
beg	begin(ning)
cont	continu(e)(ing)
cm	centimetre(s)
dec	decrease
foll	follow(ing)
g st	garter stitch, every row knit
g	gramme(s)
in	inch(es)
inc	increase
K	knit
K up	pick up and knit
K-wise	in a knitwise direction
mm	millimetre(s)
No	number
patt	pattern
psso	pass slipped stitch over
P	purl
P up	pick up and purl
P-wise	in a purlwise direction
rem	remain(ing)
rep	repeat
Rs	right side of work
sl	slip
sl st	slip stitch
st(s)	stitch(es)
st st	stocking stitch, 1 row knit, 1 row purl
tbl	through back of loop
tog	together
Ws	wrong side of work
ybk	yarn back between needles
yfwd	yarn forward between needles
yon	yarn over needle
yrn	yarn round needle

Knitting symbols

Where an asterisk, *, is shown in a row, it means that the stitches given after this sign must be repeated from that point to the end of the row, or to the last number of stitches given. Where a double asterisk is shown, **, it means that this part of the pattern will be used at a later stage on another section of the garment.

Instructions shown in square brackets, [], denote larger sizes respectively.

Instructions shown in round brackets, ( ), mean that this section of the pattern is worked on all sizes.

Knitting yarn weight conversions

25g balls	oz balls	25g balls	oz balls
1	1	13	11
3	2	14	12
4	3	15	13
5	4	16	14
6	5	17	15
7	6	18	16
8	7	19	17
9	8	21	18
10	9	22	19
12	10	23	20

Knitting needle sizes

Old British	Metric	UK Metric	American
000	10mm		15
00	9mm		13
0	8mm		12
1	7.5mm	7½mm	11
2	7mm		10½
3	6.5mm	5½mm	10
4	6mm		9
5	5.5mm	5½mm	8
6	5mm		7
7	4.5mm	4½mm	6
8	4mm		5
9	3.75mm	3¾mm	4
10	3.25mm	3¼mm	3
11	3mm		2
12	2.75mm	2¾mm	1
13	2.25mm	2¼mm	0
14	2mm		00

Circular needle chart

The following information shows the minimum number of stitches required to reach from one needle point to the other.

Tension	Needle length			
	16in/ 40cm	24in/ 60cm	32in/ 80cm	40in/ 100cm
5 sts to 1in/2.5cm	80	116	156	196
5½ sts to 1in/2.5cm	88	128	172	216
6 sts to 1in/2.5cm	96	140	188	236
6½ sts to 1in/2.5cm	104	152	204	254
7 sts to 1in/2.5cm	112	164	220	274
7½ sts to 1in/2.5cm	120	176	236	294
8 sts to 1in/2.5cm	128	188	252	314

Helping hand

If you have never knitted before or have let your skills become rusty, the following step-by-step instructions and explanatory diagrams will help you discover this craft for the first time, or will rekindle your enthusiasm.

Holding yarn and needles

Use these methods as a guide until you find a way of holding the yarn and needles which suits you. It is essential to be comfortable and relaxed or you will not produce an even fabric.

Right handed knitters should hold the yarn wound round the fingers of the right hand, in such a way as to achieve a firm fabric, (see Fig 1). The needle making the stitches is held in the right hand and the left hand needle holds the made stitches, (see Fig 2).

These illustrations are for right handed knitters. If you are left handed, prop the book up in front of you so that it is facing a mirror and work from the reflection.

fig 1 holding yarn

fig 2 holding needles

Making a slip loop

All knitting begins with a slip loop, which counts as the first cast on stitch.

To make a slip loop, take the main end from the ball of yarn across in front of the short end and use the point of the needle to pull the main length through from the back to the front and leave this loop on the needle, (see Fig 3). Draw up the main length to tighten the knot.

fig 3 slip loop

Casting on

The simplest method of casting on uses two needles. Hold the needle with the slip loop on it in your left hand and the other needle in your right hand, with the yarn wound round your fingers.

Insert the point of the right hand needle into the slip loop from the front to the back and take the yarn under and round the point, (see Fig 4). Draw the yarn through the slip loop to make a new stitch and place this stitch on the left hand needle.

*Make the next stitch by inserting the point of the right hand needle from the front to the back between the last two stitches on the left hand needle, (see Fig 5). Take the yarn under and round the point of the right hand needle and draw the yarn through to make another stitch. Place this stitch on the left hand needle.

Continue repeating from the * until you have cast on the required number of stitches.

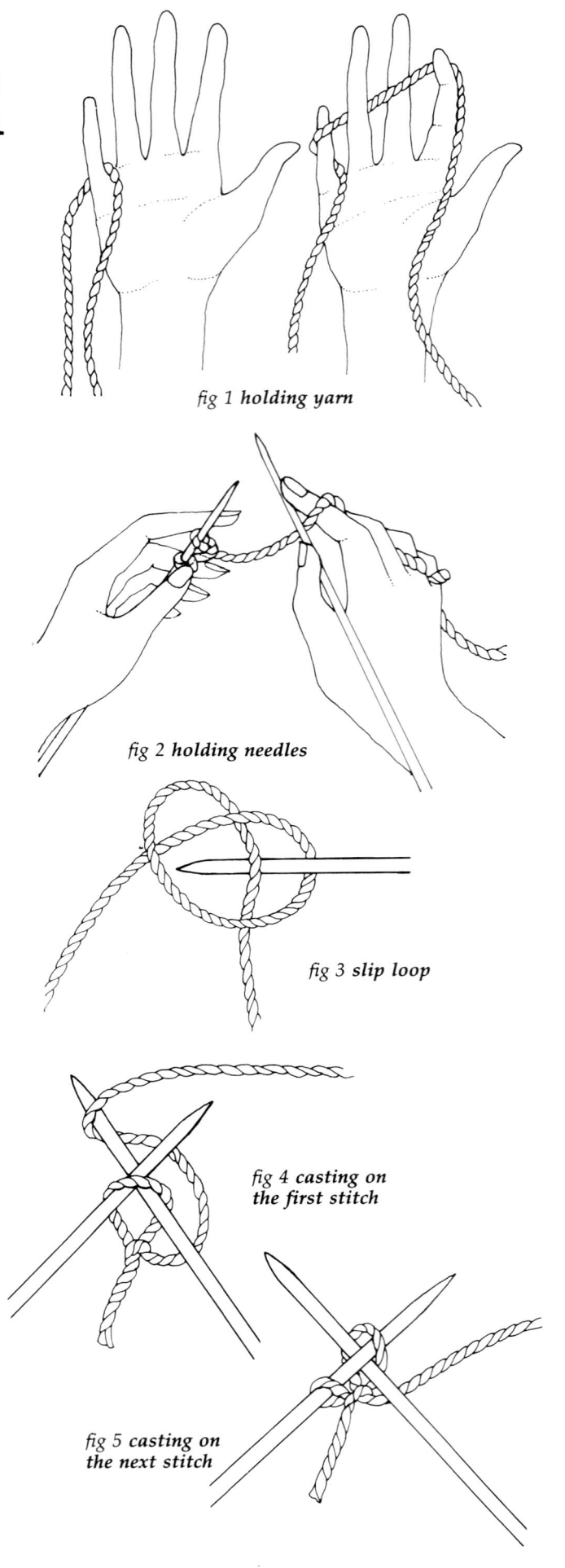

fig 4 casting on the first stitch

fig 5 casting on the next stitch

To knit stitches

To knit the first row after casting on, hold the needle containing the cast on stitches in your left hand and the yarn and spare needle in your right hand.

*Insert the point of the right hand needle through the first stitch on the left hand needle from the front to the back. Holding the yarn at the back of the work, take it under and over the point of the right hand needle and draw a loop through the stitch on the left hand needle, (see Fig 6). Keep this newly made stitch on the right hand needle and allow the stitch knitted into to drop off the left hand needle. One stitch has been knitted.

Repeat this action from the * into each stitch until all the stitches have been worked on to the right hand needle. One row has been knitted. To work the next row, transfer the needle holding the stitches to your left hand, so that the yarn is again in the correct position at the beginning of the row.

Working consecutive knitted rows in this way produces the fabric called 'garter stitch', which is closely-textured and ridged.

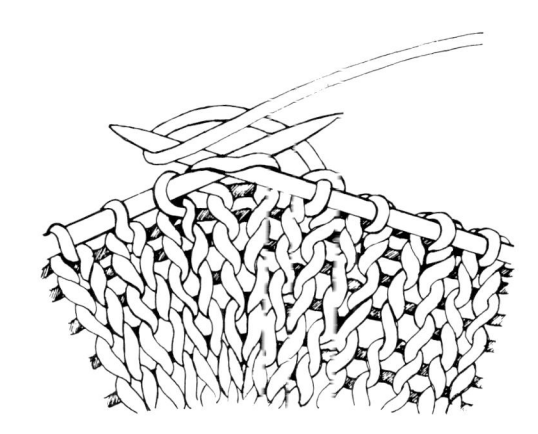

fig 6 to knit stitches

To purl stitches

Hold the needle containing the cast on, or knitted stitches in your left hand and the yarn and spare needle in your right hand.

*Insert the point of the right hand needle through the first stitch on the left hand needle from the right to the left. Holding the yarn at the front of the work, take it over and round the point of the right hand needle and draw a loop through the stitch on the left hand needle, (see Fig 7). Keep this newly made stitch on the right hand needle and allow the stitch purled into to drop off the left hand needle. One stitch has been purled.

Repeat this action from the * into each stitch until all the stitches have been worked on to the right hand needle. One row has been purled. To work the next row, transfer the needle holding the stitches to your left hand, so that the yarn is again in the correct position at the beginning of the row.

Knitting the first (right side) row and purling the second (wrong side) row, and continuing to alternate the rows in this way produces stocking stitch, the smoothest of all knitted fabrics. The purl side of this fabric is referred to as 'reversed stocking stitch'.

fig 7 to purl stitches

To shape by increasing

Where instructions state that one stitch is to be increased at the beginning, end, or at each end of a particular row as a means of shaping, the easiest method is to work twice into a stitch, thus making two out of one.

To make a stitch at the beginning of a knit row, work the first stitch in the usual way but do not allow the stitch to drop off the left hand needle. Instead, insert the right hand needle into the back loop of the same stitch and knit into it again, (see Fig. 8).

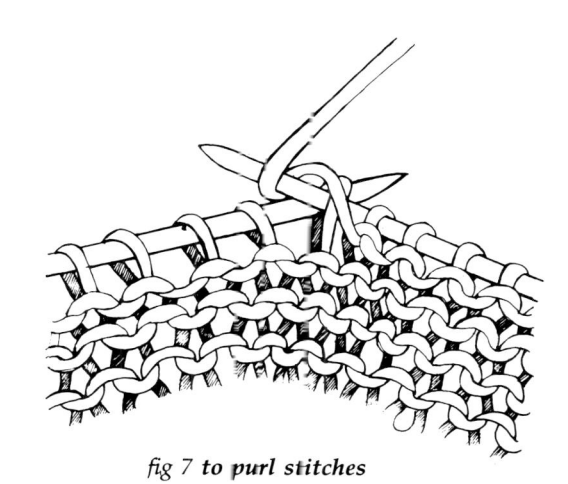

fig 8 increasing a knit stitch

To make a stitch at the end of a knit row, work until two stitches remain on the left hand needle. Increase in the next stitch as given for the beginning of the row, then work the last stitch in the usual way to keep the edge straight.

To make a stitch at the beginning of a purl row, work the first stitch in the usual way but do not allow the stitch to drop off the left hand needle. Instead, insert the right hand needle into the back loop of the same stitch but from the left to the right, and purl into it again, (see Fig 9).

To make a stitch at the end of a purl row, work until two stitches remain on the left hand needle. Increase in the next stitch as given for the beginning of the row, then work the last stitch in the usual way to keep the edge straight.

Decorative eyelet increasing

This method forms an eyelet hole in the fabric and is the basis of all aran lace knitting. Instead of knitting into a stitch to make an extra one, the yarn is taken over or round the needle to increase a stitch and this stitch is compensated for by decreasing a stitch later on in the pattern sequence.

To make a stitch between two knitted stitches, bring the yarn forward between the needles, then take it back over the top of the right hand needle ready to knit the next stitch, (see Fig. 10). This is called 'yarn forward'.

To make a stitch between a purled and knitted stitch, the yarn is already at the front of the work and should be carried over the top of the right hand needle ready to knit the next stitch, (see Fig 11). This is called 'yarn over (or on) needle'.

To make a stitch between a knitted and a purled stitch, bring the yarn forward between the needles to the front of the work, take it over the top of the right hand needle and round between the needles again ready to purl the next stitch, (see Fig 12). This is called 'yarn round needle'.

This method is also used to make a stitch between two purled stitches, noting that the yarn is already at the front of the work to begin, and should be taken over the top of the right hand needle and round between the needles ready to purl the next stitch.

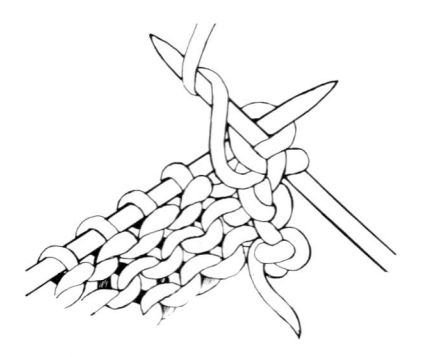

fig 9 increasing a purl stitch

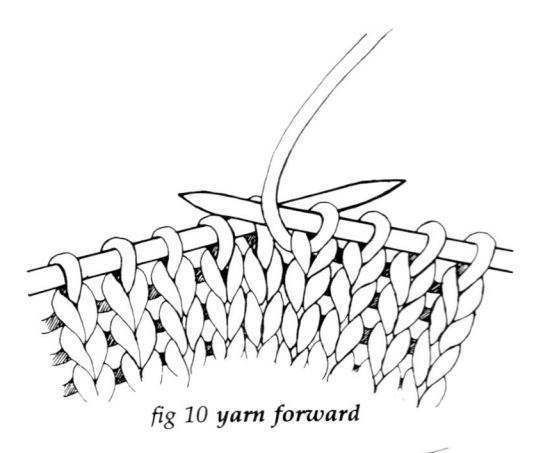

*fig 10 **yarn forward***

*fig 11 **yarn over needle***

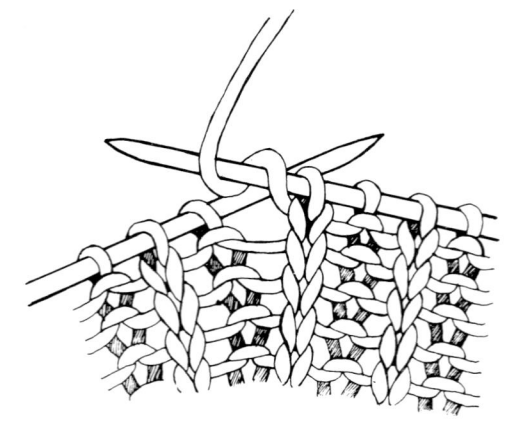

*fig 12 **yarn round needle***

To shape by decreasing

Where instructions state that one stitch is to be decreased at the beginning, end, or at each end of a particular row as a means of shaping, the easiest method is to work two stitches together, thus making one out of two.

To decrease a stitch at the beginning of a knit row, insert the point of the right hand needle from the front to the back through the first two stitches on the left hand needle, instead of through one stitch, and knit them together in the usual way, allowing both stitches to drop off the left hand needle, (see Fig 13).

To decrease a stitch at the end of a knit row, work until three stitches remain on the left hand needle. Decrease in the next two stitches as given for the beginning of the row, then work the last stitch in the usual way to keep the edge straight.

The methods for decreasing a stitch at the beginning or end of a purl row are the same as for a knit row, but the decreased stitches are purled together, inserting the right hand needle from right to left through two stitches.

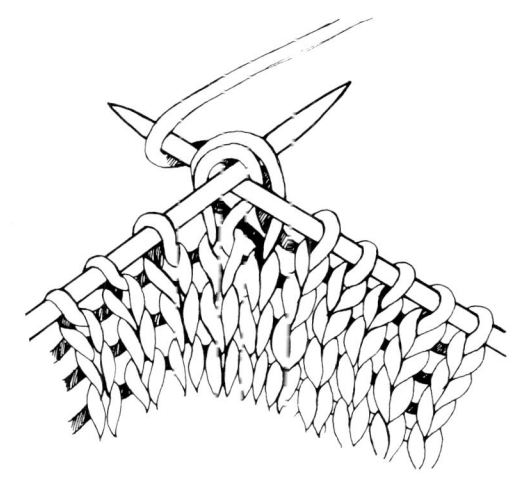

fig 13 decreasing one stitch

Casting off

This method is used to stop the stitches unravelling at the end of a completed section of knitting, or for certain areas of shaping in a section, such as necklines and shoulders. When casting off, make sure that the stitches are worked in the correct pattern sequence before they are cast off, or you will spoil the appearance of the fabric and make seaming more difficult.

To cast off stitches at the beginning of a row, work the first two stitches in pattern and leave them on the right hand needle. *Insert the point of the left hand needle into the first of the stitches worked on to the right hand needle and lift it over the top of the second stitch and off the needle, leaving one stitch on the right hand needle, (see Fig 14). Work the next stitch in pattern and leave it on the right hand needle and continue from the * until the correct number of stitches have been cast off.

If casting off is at the end of a piece of knitting, break off the yarn, draw it through the remaining stitch on the right hand needle and pull it up securely. If stitches have been cast off as a means of shaping, continue in pattern to the end of the row, noting that the stitch on the right hand needle now counts as one of the remaining stitches.

To cast off stitches in the middle of a row, work in pattern until the position for the shaping is reached, continue as given for the beginning of the row until the required number of stitches have been cast off. Pattern to the end of the row, noting that the stitch on the right hand needle now counts as one of the remaining stitches.

To cast off stitches at the end of a row, work in pattern until the number of stitches to be cast off remain on the left hand needle. Cast off these stitches and fasten off as given for the beginning of the row. To continue working on the remaining stitches, rejoin the yarn again to the beginning of the next row.

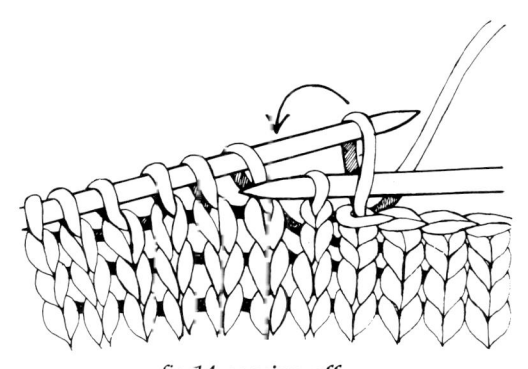

fig 14 casting off

Knitting tension

Knitting is an easy craft to master but you will not become a proficient exponent until you understand the importance of obtaining the correct tension given for a design. Many knitters believe this term means achieving an even fabric, but this is not so, although it certainly contributes to the appearance of your knitting.

The word 'tension' refers to the number of stitches and rows to a given measurement, usually 4in (10cm), which have been achieved by the *designer* of the garment, using the yarn and needle size quoted in the instructions. Without doubt, correct tension is the factor which makes the difference between successful and calamitous results, as it controls the size and shape of the design.

Each yarn manufacturer gives a recommended tension and needle size on the ball band of the qualities they produce, but this is only a guide to obtaining a *stocking stitch* fabric which is neither too tight nor too loose. As soon as you begin to work in a stitch pattern, however, this basic tension will no longer apply and the tension given in the designer's instructions will differ from those given on the ball band.

Whether you are a novice or an experienced knitter, each time you begin to knit a garment it is vital to first work a tension sample, using the correct yarn and needle size given in the instructions, to ensure that you obtain the same number of stitches and rows quoted under the 'Tension' heading. Some people naturally knit more tightly, or loosely than others and everyone differs in the way they control the yarn and needles. To begin with, there is no such thing as an 'average' tension and as you gain experience, your tension may alter with your progress.

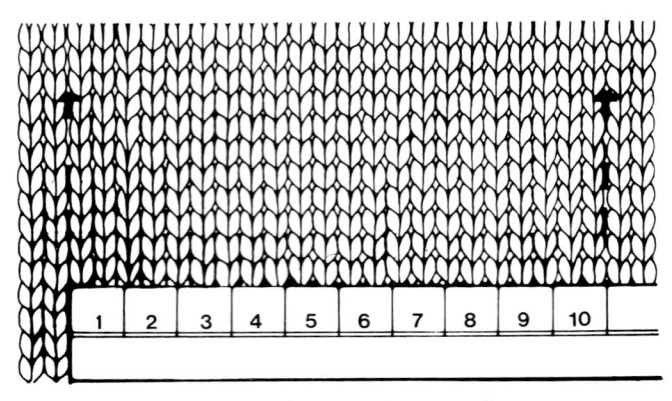

fig 15 checking tension sample

To adjust knitting tension

To adjust your tension, simply change needle sizes and work another sample. If your original sample measures *more* than the size given you are working too *loosely* and you must change to a size smaller needles. If your original sample measures *less* than the size given you are working too *tightly* and must change to a size larger needles. Experiment with different sizes until you can obtain the correct tension—it doesn't matter how many times you have to change needles. Most garments are knitted so that the stitches form the width tension and the rows the length. If you have to choose between obtaining one or the other, the width tension is the most vital and length can be adjusted by working more or less rows to achieve the given measurement.

Always use new yarn to work each tension sample. If you keep unravelling the same yarn it will become stretched and will not give an accurate tension. If you are substituting another yarn for the one given in the instructions, it is even more essential to check your tension. In using a different yarn from the original quoted, you may also find that the amount required will vary and you may not be able to produce the texture of the original fabric.

To check knitting tension

Always work a sample of at least 4in (10cm) using the yarn, needle size and stitch pattern given in the instructions. If the tension is given as 22 stitches and 30 rows to 4in (10cm) worked in stocking stitch on No 8 (4mm) needles, cast on at least 26 stitches and work 34 rows, to enable you to measure the sample accurately.

Lay the completed sample on a flat surface and pin it down at the corners, without stretching it. Place a firm ruler across the knitting and mark out the number of stitches and rows you have obtained to 4in (10cm) with pins, (see Fig 15). Count the stitches and rows very carefully, as even half a stitch makes a great deal of difference to the finished size of the garment.

Blocking and pressing

Many of the yarns available today are completely ruined if they are pressed, so do check the spinner's recommendation on the ball band.

Where pressing is advised, it is easier if each section is first pinned out to the correct measurements and shape — this is particularly important in lace knitting. This is referred to as 'blocking', (see Fig 16). Use a firm, well-padded surface and place each section right side down on to this, securing each corner with rustless pins. Gently pat the section into size and shape, making sure that the side edges are

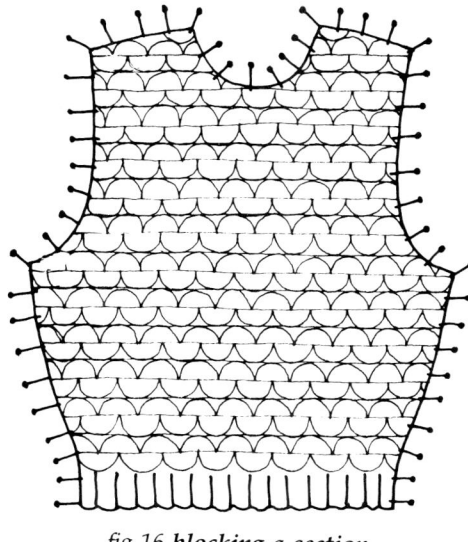

fig 16 blocking a section

straight and that the stitches and rows run in straight lines. Check that the measurements are the same as those given in the instructions, or as shown in the pattern pieces diagram. Now pin the section evenly to the padded surface round all the edges.

To press each section, have the iron at the correct temperature and a clean dry, or damp, cloth as directed in the instructions or on the ball band. Place the cloth over the section and gently press the whole area of the iron down on top of the cloth, then lift it up again. Do not run the iron over the surface of the cloth as you would if you were ironing, as this will stretch the knitting. Press each area in this way and when the section is completed, remove the pins and lay it aside ready for seaming.

Making up garments

When the various sections have been completed and pressed, it is the final seaming and finishing touches which will give your garments a professional look.

Seaming

To join the sections together, the best method to use is a back stitch seam. Unless it is very thick, or highly-textured, the yarn used to knit the garment should be used for seaming.

Place the right sides of each piece together and sew along the wrong side of the fabric, about ¼in (0.5cm) in from the edge. Thread a length of yarn into a blunt-ended sewing needle. Working from right to left along the seam, secure the yarn at the end with a few small running stitches.

*With the sewing needle at the back of the work, move it to the left about the width of one knitted stitch, push it through to the front of the work and pull the yarn through. Take the needle across the front of the work from left to right and insert it through the fabric at the end of the last stitch, then pull the yarn through, (see Fig 17).

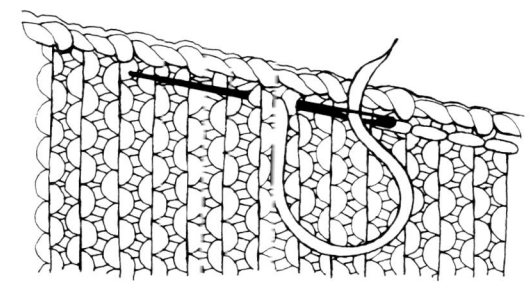

fig 17 back stitch seam

Continue working from the * in this way until the seam is completed, then fasten off at the end with a few small running stitches.

Picking up stitches

Necklines and borders need to be neatened with edges applied after the garment has been seamed. To do this, stitches must be picked up evenly along the edge, knitted in the stitch pattern given in the instructions and then cast off. Have the right side of the fabric facing you.

*Insert the needle from the back to the front, either under both loops at the top of cast off stitches, or between the loops of the first stitch in from the edge of the knitting. Wind the yarn round the point of the needle as when knitting a stitch and pull this loop through, leaving a stitch on the needle, (see Fig 18).

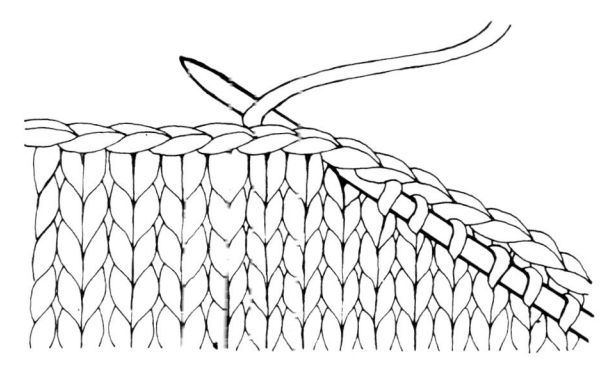

fig 18 picking up stitches

Continue working from the * in this way until the required number of stitches have been picked up, then complete the edge as given in the instructions.

31

OTHER KNITTING TITLES

HAVE YOU ANY WOOL?
The Creative Use of Yarn
by Jan Messent
A new concept in knitting and crochet, Jan Messent breaks fresh ground with stimulating project ideas to encourage readers to extend the boundaries of their work: a plate of vegetables; a costume gallery; a collection of tube figures and wall-hangings to name just a few!

WOOL 'N MAGIC
by Jan Messent
Wool 'n Magic gives a completely new slant on knitting, crochet and embroidery. You can use your skills to make unique garments and items, combining all three techniques and discover a world of texture, fabric and colour to delight your imagination. Within these pages you will also find ideas and designs for picture knitting, a patchwork town and landscapes, colour experiments using nature as a source and many more fascinating projects.

KNIT A FANTASY STORY
by Jan Messent
Using oddments of wool and other simple materials create your own enchanted world of witches and wizards, fairies and goblins or knit a charming collection of farm animals. Hours of fun for children and grown-ups alike.

KNITTED GARDENS
by Jan Messent
This book will delight both knitters and garden-lovers alike and is ideal as a single or group project. It begins with a 'know-how' section of basic and useful knitting stitches and then gives detailed instructions for creating a variety of unusual gardens. These include a three-dimensional 'Friary Garden', 'Cottage Row', a garden bedspread and vegetable cushion, the 'Garden Centre', the 'Seed Catalogue' and, finally, 'Gardeners and Friends' which includes garden birds, a hedgehog, a rabbit and a squirrel.

THE KNITTED FARMYARD
by Hannelore Wernhard
The Knitted Farmyard gives instructions for knitting and crocheting a complete three-dimensional farmyard, with fields, trees, cows, hens, pigs, the farmer and his family. All the figures are based on pipe-cleaners, oddments of knitting yarns and embroidery threads.

KNIT AN ENCHANTED CASTLE
by Jan Messent
Enter a world of enchantment and create an enchanted castle where witches, wizards, unicorns, dragons and knights on horseback live. With a little imagination, oddments of yarn and some knitting needles, you can create your own fairytale.

KNITTED CATS
by Joy Gammon
From the three basic patterns shown in this book you can create your own version of the ideal pet. Whether your preference runs to a macho moggie, or a sophisticated Siamese, these fluffy knitted felines make wonderful toys, cushions and companions.

KNITTED GNOMES AND FAIRIES
by Jan Messent
Jan Messent shows how to knit a delightful selection of leprechauns, characters from 'A Midsummer Night's Dream', brownies, elves and fairies. Based on wire figures, each model has its own knitted clothing, wings, wands, hats and scarves.

KNIT THE CHRISTMAS STORY
by Jan Messent
This three-dimensional Nativity scene can be made from the simplest materials by beginners and more experienced knitters. The familiar and well-loved figures are all there, with angels, shepherds, sheep, ox and ass, and the three kings worshipping round the crib with Mary and Joseph.

KNITTED DOGS
by Joy Gammon
Knit a sheepdog, or a shaggy Afghan. Cuddle up with a loveable mongrel. The choice of breed, size and colour is all yours. From three basic patterns you can knit as many as you like. If you get overrun they make marvelous presents.

If you are interested in the above books or any other of the art and craft titles published by Search press please send for a free colour catalogue to:
Search Press Ltd, Dept B, Wellwood, North Farm Road, Tunbridge Wells, Kent TN2 3DR.